NOT SO
FAR
FROM
HOME

NOT SO FAR FROM HOME

Returning To The Heart Of God

JOHN TIMMERMAN

Victor®

The Bible Teacher's Teacher

COOK COMMUNICATIONS MINISTRIES
Colorado Springs, Colorado • Paris, Ontario
KINGSWAY COMMUNICATIONS LTD
Eastbourne, England

Victor® is an imprint of
Cook Communications Ministries, Colorado Springs, CO 80918
Cook Communications, Paris, Ontario
Kingsway Communications, Eastbourne, England

NOT SO FAR FROM HOME
© 2006 by John H. Timmerman

Cover Design: Greg Jackson, Thinkpen Design, llc

First Printing, 2006
Printed in the United States of America

1 2 3 4 5 6 7 8 9 10 Printing/Year 11 10 09 08 07 06

ISBN: 0-7814-4256-7

LCCN: 2006920278

The Ezra-Nehemiah Chronology

626–586: Jeremiah (in Judah)
605: Nebuchadnezzar defeats the Egyptians at Carchemish;
First deportation into exile includes Daniel
605–562: Nebuchadnezzar rules
597: King Jehoiakim taken into exile; Jehoiachin rules
three months; Nebuchadnezzar attacks Jerusalem
597: Second deportation includes Ezekiel
593–571: Ezekiel prophesies in exile
586: Babylonians destroy Jerusalem and the temple;
Third deportation
559–530: Cyrus rules as Persian king
539: Cyrus captures Babylon
538: Zerubbabel and Sheshbazzar return to Judah
538: Zechariah returns from Babylon to Judah
537: Israelites rebuild the altar
536: Work on the temple begins (foundations)
530–522: Cambyses rules
530–520: Work on the temple ceases until restarted by
Darius
522–486: Darius rules
520: Haggai delivers four prophecies in exile; Zechariah
begins prophesying (final prophecy ca. 480)
516: Work on the temple is completed
486–464: Xerxes I (Ahasuerus) rules; Esther serves as
Ahasuerus's queen
464–423: Artaxerxes rules
458: Ezra arrives in Jerusalem
445: Nehemiah arrives in Jerusalem
445: The wall is rebuilt
438: Nehemiah returns to Persia

Contents

ॐ

Introduction

ॐ

The gray morning light shifted slowly. Standing in the deep valley, he began to distinguish the shadows that rimmed the cliffs.

Ridges rose in the distance, surrounding him like the rim of a cauldron. The western walls, lit now by the sun, gave off splashes of pure white and veins of red, as if they were all ablaze. A holy place.

It lay before him like a vast coliseum, he the only spectator. He could imagine wars waged here across the plains. He stood watching, alertly waiting for any sign of revelation. The overhead sky was now the pale blue that foretold intense heat. Not a breath of wind stirred.

Sweat furrowed under his thick black hair and ran down his back. His brow and chest grew damp. He waited. All he saw were shadows fleeing as the sun worked its way down the fiery walls.

It was not the first time Ezekiel had been called to a holy place to await the Lord's revelation. He was a Levite, and he had assumed his place in the priesthood on his thirtieth

birthday. Now he was thirty-three, lean as a staff, his thick
black hair tied not in the old way around his ears but falling
loose down his shoulders. That didn't matter. His ears were
tuned to hearing the Voice, his eyes to seeing the revelation.
Not exactly a priest, this Ezekiel—for without a temple there
could not be a priest. It had been a long time since anyone
had been installed into that sacred community.

Now word had come in this year 586 BC, and to this land
of exile, that the sacred temple in Jerusalem and that holy
city itself had been burned to ruins. All the old ways, he
thought, were like grains of sand blown before the wind.

A vagabond priest, then. A stranger in a strange land
with no centering point. He knew well that in some areas of
the exile the older priests struggled to keep the traditions
alive in the people's minds. But not him. If not a priest—a
prophet. The visions wouldn't desert him. Indeed, they
wouldn't leave him alone. So once again he found himself in
this anticipation of vision, feeling the heat of the new day
rise through breathless air, waiting for what was to come.

Now the sun seared Ezekiel's face. Yet he stood watching.
No wind. No shade. Perfect silence.

Almost in a flash, as if drawing back a curtain, sunlight
flooded the valley floor.

Ezekiel nearly sank to his knees. He thought they were
stones at first. Some straight like sticks. Some rounded. All
burned white and dry by the sun. There was no mistaking it.
This was a place of the dead. Bones scattered beyond his seeing. Heaps of bones, wind blown and piled against each
other like dried weeds. His jaw set in a taut line. He squinted
against the blazing sight of overwhelming destruction. Why,
of all places, did the Voice take me here?

The Voice spoke to him and he walked, shuffling among
the bones. He walked a long time, yet the white carpet

unfurled ever onward. Suddenly his own throat was parched with thirst. The sun stood overhead like a blister in the white sky.

The Voice spoke, "Son of man, can these bones live?" What? These desiccated twigs? These ... these dried up old broken bits and pieces of bone?

Ezekiel—the prophet—knew better: "O Sovereign Lord, you alone know." You alone.

This is the prophecy: The Lord will knit these bones together, bind them with tendon and muscle, clothe them in flesh, and breathe life into them.

Ezekiel did not hesitate. Maybe for a split second the thought entered his mind—impossible! Madness! Maybe he flinched an eye, looking for a way out of the valley. But he did not leave. He prophesied to these dried sticks of bones.

For the first time the absolute silence of the valley broke. It came first as a slight rustling, the faintest whisper as dry bones slid across dry earth. Then louder. The bones clacked together in place, all across the vast valley. The noise filled the plain, like drumsticks beating upon each other. *Snap! Snap!*

Then a more soothing sound. The bones wrapped together in tendon and flesh—a re-creation of human life. But it was not complete yet.

Still missing from that re-creation was the power of God to grant new life altogether. It appeared in Genesis when God breathed life into the first man: "The Lord God formed the man from the dust of the ground and breathed into his nostrils the breath of life, and the man became a living being" (2:7). It came again with new life for all believers at Pentecost (see Acts 2). So it is here. Ezekiel prophesied at the Lord's command. Suddenly the still air was beaten by howling wind, coming from all directions, swirling down upon the lifeless shapes on the valley floor.

But lifeless no longer, for the breath of life was in them. They stood. They stretched. They ran, testing muscles made anew. They laughed and sang with the new breath in newly made lungs.

The revelation was not for Ezekiel's sake alone. Right from the start, Ezekiel acknowledged God's absolute knowledge and power: "O Sovereign LORD, you alone know" (37:3). Rather, it was for the Israelites in exile, those who lament that "Our bones are dried up and our hope is gone" (37:11). They felt separated from God, twisted and abandoned in this strange land. Surrounded by other gods, their memory of the true traditions began to recede. They were, as people of God, drying out.

Here is God's promise to these people: "I will put my Spirit in you and you will live" (37:14). They would come alive to be led once again out of bondage by the mighty hand of God. But who would lead them home?

Ezekiel was a prophet, not a leader of people. He was given visions, not the power to carry them out. Now the people needed leaders, also filled with the Spirit of God, to bring the breath of new life to them. Who could make them a people of God again? And how? Again, God had an answer already prepared in two remarkable leaders of the Israelites.

Upon first glance, the two men couldn't have seemed more different. One, Ezra, was revered by the people, a man who kept the Law and knew the traditions of service to God even while in exile. Although unable to offer the sacrifices while in exile, Ezra was in the lineage of Aaron the high priest. He had studied the Law carefully. He was a shrewd, intelligent man, gifted in speech and insight. He was a man of Israel, one of the great family.

By contrast, Nehemiah was a cupbearer to King Arta-xerxes, the one entrusted by the king to sample his drink in case it was poisoned. Nehemiah was accustomed to royalty, to courtly custom and tradition. Indeed, he was a favorite of the king. As one of the king's primary courtiers, he was likely a eunuch—his only family his fellows in the court. Yet he was a man of powerful emotions.

Contrasting details are only accidental, the way one person becomes a farmer and the other a secretary. The similarities in the two men are far more profound, for they measure the spirit of life within them. Both men possessed an undaunted courage—Ezra to lead the returnees from exile across a thousand miles of wasteland; Nehemiah to plead the cause of his people before a king whose single word could have him slain. Both possessed fierce dedication. When opposition arose, they stood resolute. Both were led by the Spirit of the Lord to sound decisions, and both based their actions upon God's Word alone. In short, they provided perfect examples of restoring an exiled community, of making them once again the people of God.

We find it difficult to comprehend the lostness of the Israelites in captivity. Ripped from their homeland, scattered in a foreign land, they longed for a way out and a way back. The sheer number of people involved in this national scattering is overwhelming. But suffering is always, finally, individual. The loneliness drapes down in a person's own mind, like a thick curtain shutting out joy. Sometimes we feel like dried bones in a hot valley, waiting for the Spirit wind. None of us escapes suffering.

How do we find our own way out of lostness and suffering then? We need a guide. In God's marvelous working in these brief, and frequently overlooked, chapters of the Israelites' life, we find one such guide. It is as if God speaks directly to us out of the pages of his history saying, "Hold on.

My guidance is sure. The walls can be rebuilt. You can dance with joy again as persons of God."

The first brave caravan of Israelites returned from captivity in Persia after traveling hundreds of miles across desert and through mountains. When they looked on the ruins of the sacred city, their hopes must have seemed hollow and brittle. The place was in desolation. How does one begin to reconstruct life out of the wasteland? That is precisely the question so many believers also ask today as they seek out answers in the crush of this world of exile.

We all have a longing for intimacy with God. We, too, long for a sacred place, somewhere we can lay down our burden, receive forgiveness, and gain hope for the future. Out of the ruined walls we want to rebuild a rock-solid faith that grants joy. As did those Israelites, we will see that the struggle for joy is not a matter of skipping along with happy laughter. Joy takes work and commitment, even confrontation with darkness. But joy is also that thunderous power of God revitalizing our spiritual selves. It is the power against which no darkness can stand, and it leads us beyond incidental laughter to dancing on the walls of a new life. In that discovery, which is nothing less than the whole of the Christian life, these people out of the ancient past have lessons to teach us.

To accept those lessons and to be directed by them requires some hard confrontation with ourselves, however. So too with the Israelites. They must have looked at their options and wondered whether it wouldn't be easier just to stay in Persia. Indeed it would have been. The consequence, however, would be continued severance from the Spirit of God that brings life and joy—no matter the circumstances.

Ezra and Nehemiah set a model for the people of God in their time. The effectiveness of that model as a pathway to becoming the people of God has in no way diminished. In fact, one finds careful steps along the path. Step one consists of remembering who we are before God. We must confront ourselves and discover that we are persons in need of forgiveness. More important, we must learn to live as forgiven persons.

The second step moves from confrontation with who we are to drawing close to God himself. The first task of the returning Israelites was not to construct new living quarters, nor to build a temple, nor to worry about a livelihood. It was to build an altar, a place to be close to God.

The new relationship, moreover, needs sustenance. Thus the third step to becoming people of God is to renew spiritual foundations. For the Israelites, the task consisted of rebuilding the temple so that the ceremonies and sacrifices of their faith might endure. For us, no less, the pathway to personhood in God consists of reestablishing certain patterns in order to remain in fellowship with him.

Even with these spiritual foundations erected, however, one faces the temptation to rely upon ceremonies and laws alone as testament to faith. The fourth step, then, is learning to live an authentic faith, one that manifests daily our relationship with God.

To be authentically faithful is to live in fidelity. But what exactly does this mean? At the time of some personal, inward storm that buffets our faith, or when external events pummel us, we want to understand, as the fifth step, how to be people of fidelity.

Sometimes during those very storms we long simply for a quiet place—a retreat from the world with its confounding puzzles. Yet the people of God are called to be active in the world. This is a hard saying, for this is God's world and he has called each of us to redeem it. The sixth step, then, is to be people of action.

What then? Do we keep fighting the battles, slogging from one challenge to another? That is not the Ezra/Nehemiah model at all. The true glory of their remarkable journey is that it arrives as celebration, in the case of the Israelites, a joyous celebration with people literally dancing on the walls. Here too is the remarkable promise of our journey. The people of God are finally, thoroughly, people of joy.

CHAPTER 1

Living in Exile

Reading: Deuteronomy 30

The story truly begins in the very earliest stages of the Hebrew nation.

Abram, the first person in the Bible to be called a Hebrew, received a surprising promise from God during a night vision. Abram and his wife, Sarai, were an aged couple, and childless. Yet God led Abram out under the night sky and told him: "Look up at the heavens and count the stars—if indeed you can count them.... So shall your offspring be" (Gen. 15:5).

Modern astronomers tell us that about eight thousand stars are visible in the darkness of a Middle Eastern night. Tallying the number isn't the point, however. To the unaided eye, the stars seem to shift, to grow in brightness and diminish as the nerves in the retina struggle to take it all in and make some sense of the dazzle. They may as well be countless. So it was for Abram—an astronomical bewilderment of a promise.

Two other surprises enter into this story of Abram's promised offspring. First, Abram was a nomad. He really had no country to call his own, no home for these offspring. His herding group was large, including more than three hundred men trained for battle, but they followed the seasons and the landscape to feed their flocks and herds.

The second surprise comes from what must have been a completely baffling statement from God: "Know for certain that your descendents will be strangers in a country not their own, and they will be enslaved and mistreated four hundred years" (15:13).

Here's a strange twist of plot. Aged Abram and Sarai are promised countless descendents. But they have no home except the territories they wander through for those descendants to live. Worse, eventually these offspring will spend four hundred years in exiled slavery.

One could say that from early on the Israelites became experts in the art of exile. They suffered it often.

The years passed and a horror descended on the land. Drought browned the landscape. Day by day the molten sun scorched every living thing. Starving people scrabbled for food, their children sank into the listless stupor of hunger. Animals tottered along with ribs protruding from tight hides. The whole land lay clenched in the fist of famine.

But in Egypt, one of Abram's offspring named Joseph had stored enough grain to feed all his kinsfolk. With fear and gratitude, Joseph's father, the old patriarch Jacob, his brothers, and all their families carted their belongings from the parched landscape of Canaan down to Egypt. Surely, Joseph and the plenty of Egypt were their deliverers, their salvation.

Then salvation turned to slavery. The Israelites longed for their true home, and that longing itself constitutes the heartache of exile. Interestingly, the Latin root for the word *exile* literally means "to wander." To live in exile is to wander, without any sense of right direction, without any familiar markers of home territory, and without hope. Exiles are both powerless on their own and subjected to the enslaving whims of those who hold power over them.

From salvation to slavery—it still seems to be the tendency of humanity to wander into exile.

From slavery to salvation—it is still the fundamental message of the Bible. It is the bottom line of Christianity.

Yet we often choose, willingly, of our own design, to live in the darkness of exile.

This business of wandering without direction affected me in a new way recently. Isaac Newton defined the force of gravity. What he didn't tell us is that as one grows older the force increases. Knees pop strangely when one gets up from the floor. Parts of the body suddenly sag. Sometimes the body emits creaking sounds like loose floorboards. When gravitationally challenged in this way, it helps to hang on to the doorframe with one hand to put pants on. This further force of gravity even seems to pull people's hair right out of their heads.

Before my knees succumbed to this strange force, I was a runner. I especially liked to run on hot summer days during my lunch break. The sun was a high brassy ball; the air on back roads so pure it seemed to heal the heart.

If one is a runner in Michigan, however, challenges appear. In the autumn, rains splash across fallen leaves like a slick oil spill. Anytime from November to April, snow and ice can clog the sidewalks. A runner then escapes to a gym and, with a fair degree of shame, turns to a treadmill. No more sunny skies and grassy fields. Instead, echoes of grunts and groans, and sweaty bodies packed shoulder to shoulder. It's like exercising in a cattle feed lot.

If that weren't indignity enough, there is the treadmill itself. Sure, you can adjust the speed and factor in fake hills. But no matter how hard you run, you never really get anywhere. Except to the end of your allotted time. Then you stand there dizzy and soaked with sweat, but you really haven't gone anywhere. Motion without direction. Ah, for those blue skies and a fierce sun, the smell of mown grass and flowers as you pass by.

Exile is a bit like the treadmill. People wander without getting anywhere. Their lives lack direction and eventually, they lack hope. At times I feel precisely like I am living in exile. Running on a treadmill without really getting anywhere. Wandering from moment to moment, from task to task, without a whole lot of direction or hope. At such times, I also feel fear running hard at my sweaty back, catching up way too quickly.

The writer of the epistle to the Hebrews aims to identify the divine nature and also the human task of Jesus. The writer's first task, then, is to define the "exact representation of his being" as Son of God and Son of Man (Heb. 1:3). By so doing, the writer first sets Jesus apart from all other heavenly beings, identified here as the angels.

The sweeping majesty of this first chapter of Hebrews stuns me each time I read it. Oddly, it also reminds me of what I've lost—a reverent sense of the power and majesty of angels themselves. Our culture has been seduced by the benign angelic creatures of television. I have to remind myself that in Scripture, angels bear the authority of God and that their power comes from him alone.

Consequently, in countless scriptural references, the first words spoken by angels are "Be not afraid." We have simply domesticated them to good buddies we'd like to have on our side. Similarly, as we tromp along our life's treadmill, it also seems that we have lost our fear of God. Therein lies our exile. The Bible is peppered with references to "Fear the Lord your God" (see, for example, Lev. 19:14; Deut. 6:13; Josh.

24:14; Ps. 2:11; Prov. 3:7; Eccl. 12:13; Rev. 14:7). But what is meant by "fear of the Lord"; how do we reconcile it with the angels' command, "Be not afraid"?

Spiritual fear is a matter of what we set first in our lives. Fear is a positioning of ourselves in *reverence* and *awe* before a supreme God. Fear says that you, God, are my reason for living and the end for all my actions. You, God, are my direction and my pattern for living my life with meaning and hope.

Fear requires *submission*. We take ourselves off the wandering treadmill of exile and of living for our own sake. In fear, we give ourselves to God who leads us and supports us in the path of a meaningful life.

Fear is ultimately *liberating*. By giving ourselves to God, we receive ourselves wholly. In fear we believe, as God said to Jeremiah (29:11), that we have a future and a hope. This is not a future we find by scurrying around on the treadmill like so many mice. This future and hope are already given to us before our world began (Ps. 139), and await our discovery as we turn our eyes from ourselves to our God. That is the first step out of exile—from worry to wonder, from wandering to walking with the Lord at our side.

But a different kind of fear also intrudes here—the fear that we are unworthy even to long for God's presence. In many ways it is much more comfortable to live in exile. We duck into the shadows and hope that God won't find our messy little lives.

In C. S. Lewis's fantasy *The Great Divorce,* pilgrims from hell file into a bus for a cosmic ride to the fringes of heaven. The dilemma starts with boarding, for they pass from the bleak darkness of hell into a well-lit bus. As he boards, the narrator "glanced around the bus. Though the windows were closed, and soon muffed, the bus was full of light. It was a cruel light" (25). One can hide in hell, but the light of heaven reveals who we really are. In Lewis's book, we really are thin, unsubstantial beings of no account. In fact, the very grass blades of heaven stab the travelers' feet like thorns. To stand in heaven, we have to step out of ourselves. If the light is cruel at first, it leads us to a place where we are bathed in glory. If the traveler has to make the first choice to board the bus, the fact is that the bus is provided. With every choice to stand in the light after that, heaven responds with even greater clarity, grace, and finally substantiality.

It is not just a matter, however, of divine things making themselves clearer. They have been clear all along. How can God be anything *but* clarity and grace? That never changes, not from all eternity. As we choose to turn from the shadows of exile, we begin to apprehend the grace that has been there all along.

We cling to our state of exile because we grow comfortable there. Perhaps we say something like, "God made me this way. I can't help it." Or something like, "I'm happy with myself just as I am. I'm not interested in losing myself." The fact is that only by turning from self can we discover our true selves. If we give ourselves up to God, we become truly ourselves.

In his work on apologetics, *Mere Christianity,* C. S. Lewis also addressed this point. Paraphrasing the words of Jesus, Lewis writes: "Christ says 'Give me All. I don't want so much of your time and so much of your money and so much of your work: I want You. I have not come to torment your natural self, but to kill it'" (169). Is that fearful enough? But Jesus also promises that he will give us a new self instead. In fact, he will give us himself, so that his will becomes our will.

But still, turning from exile and turning toward God, which is the literal meaning of *conversion,* seems so very frightening. When we are exposed, we realize we need forgiveness. We have to come before God. As an old hymn states:

Just as I am, without one plea,
But that Thy blood was shed for me,
And that Thou bidst me come to Thee,
O Lamb of God, I come, I come.

Deep within our hearts beats a yearning for forgiveness, an overwhelming sense that our own wrong actions have separated us from God and from our fellow humans. We also long for restoration, a sense that things can be made right. Instead of exile, we want a home, a place of peace and meaningful community. Yet somehow our minds interpose reasons or fears that stifle the yearning.

Consider this analogy. All my life I have been allergic to poison ivy. If I pass within ten feet of it, something seems to leap off the plant and attach its sticky, nasty pores to my skin. As a young boy, I spent at least one week each summer swathed head to toe in calamine lotion. I was a pink, swollen monster from the deep. A bath each night, with the water as hot as I could stand it, soothed my raging flesh. Then, while I slept, my fingers responded to their primitive call and scratched through the fresh, flaking calamine, spreading the poison further. A huge, pink, tormented blob, that's what I was for at least a week every summer.

I've never outgrown the allergy. But now the course of medical treatment is clearer. When those wrists (the invariable point of first attack) begin to swell like overripe tomatoes, I rush to the doctor's office for cortisone injections. I know my need; the doctor knows the cure.

Last summer was different. I came down with my usual affliction. It started with a sprinkling of red dots along the wrists and forearms, a bit of swelling. I called the doctor, thinking to catch it early. It so happened, however, that I was now taking a strong medication for another condition. In this case the steroid drugs were "contraindicated." That's medical talk for the fact that cortisone and the other medicine didn't mix. Indeed, the mixture could be fatal. The doctor prescribed a topical, antiseptic ointment and sent me not at all merrily on my way.

The ointment might as well have been water. A placebo I didn't need. My arms blew up like Popeye with a fresh can of spinach. They blistered and broke open, soaking the bandages and medical tape that bound me shoulder to fingers. Three times a day my wife helped me change the disgusting things. After a week of this painful torment, I went back to the doctor. "I have to take the chance," I pleaded. "Give me what I need to cure this mess." He did. Both injections and topical steroids. After another week my arms were shrinking to their normal size, crisscrossed with welts and pits, but well on the way toward healing.

Without taking the fatal risk, I wouldn't have been healed. I wish I had done it sooner.

Sometimes our need rises so powerfully in us that we don't know where to turn for healing. The pain twists awfully in places we can't begin to scratch. We feel bloated with anguish. Then we have to take the great risk. Do we turn ourselves over, wholly and completely, to the Great Physician? Or do we hide our hurt under stinking, filthy bandages of our routine lives and work hard to convince ourselves that this is just the way we are?

What deters us from running back from exile toward home? As we try to capture an overview of the Israelites in exile, their fears and need for forgiveness, consider briefly some reasons that will be developed more fully in future chapters. Our first step out of exile is always the hard task of personal honesty. "*This* is precisely what I am and what I have done." It's the hardest kind of self-examination, probing deeply within, where it hurts, and unearthing the malignancy of one's sin. David had the courage to do this. After his sin with Bathsheba, he turned to God in Psalm 51:

> For I know my transgressions,
> and my sin is always before me.
> Against you, you only, have I sinned
> and done what is evil in your sight. (vv. 3–4)

If David had stopped there, however, his task would only be half done. This heartbreaking confession would simply admit him to a seat on that long mourner's bench that stretches throughout history.

David knew that he couldn't remedy his sin through his own will, even if he was one of the most powerful kings on earth. His second step, then, is to beg for forgiveness. How does he dare? Look at what he has done. He virtually raped Bathsheba. Even worse, to possess her he sent her husband, Uriah, out to battle with express directions to let him be killed. Both an adulterer and a murderer, then. He would never forget his sin, but he knew, like a pounding in his heart, that he had to be made right with God or else all is lost. He needs forgiveness—to be whole and to function as God's servant.

His prayer for forgiveness follows crucial steps. First, he begs for cleansing:

> Cleanse me with hyssop, and I will be clean;
> wash me, and I will be whiter than snow. (v. 7)

David throws himself wholly before God's power; in no way is he able to effect such radical cleansing on his own. On his own he would merely muddle along with the pain of guilt eating away at his spirit like some gross infection.

So much seems packed into those two lines of David. The meaning of the Hebrew words used here for "Cleanse me" is literally "Un-sin me." David begs to be remade as one without sin. Furthermore, hyssop was used in Old Testament times for ritual cleansing. But it was also used during the exodus to brush blood on the doorframe. At that sign, the angel of death would pass over a house (Ex. 12:21–30). We hear of hyssop again in the New Testament. When Jesus hung on the cross as the perfect sacrifice for sin, when his blood was splashed so that the angel of death would pass over his believers, he cried out, "I am thirsty." Here's the response: "A jar of wine vinegar was there, so they soaked a sponge in it, put the sponge on a stalk of the hyssop plant, and lifted it to Jesus' lips" (John 19:29). Here was our ultimate cleansing.

After his prayer for the cleansing grace of forgiveness, David begs God for restoration. He recognizes that his sin has separated him from God. Sin is that dark wedge that we pound into the relationship. Therefore, David pleads not only for forgiveness but also for a complete spiritual overhaul:

> Create in me a pure heart, O God,
> and renew a steadfast spirit within me. (v. 10)

He seeks restoration of the broken relationship, invoking the Holy Spirit's power to "restore to me the joy of your salvation" (v. 12).

Recognition and admission of one's personal sin shapes the first step to forgiveness. We cannot be forgiven unless we recognize that we need forgiveness. In the second step, one turns to God as the source of forgiveness. Sin is not a problem we can work out on our own. Isaiah said that "all our righteous acts are like filthy rags" (64:6). We have to turn those rags over to God and let him do the washing. In the third step of forgiveness we walk into a restored relationship with God. We accept his forgiveness. We believe he has forgiven us. We no longer have to walk around with stooped shoulders and faces a mile long. David declares:

> O Lord, open my lips,
> and my mouth will declare your praise. (v. 15)

There's the right attitude of a forgiven person—joy in living and praise for God. That joy is ever-elusive when we wander through the swamp of our sins. We need our feet set on steady ground to find our voices of praise.

Through his prayer, David moved from the brokenness of his spiritual exile to a renewed wholeness before God.

One way of looking at the history of exile, then, is the pattern of slavery to salvation, carried out by the power of forgiveness. Here is another way to set the pattern: chronologically. The dates are, by necessity, often approximations.

- 2000–1675 BC: The age of the patriarchs; Abram, renamed Abraham, begins the lineage of Isaac, Jacob, and Joseph.
- 1675–1325 BC: The Israelites live in slavery in Egypt; under Moses they wander in the desert.
- 1225–1050 BC: The Israelites are led by the judges.
- 1050–1010 BC: Saul reigns as Israel's first king.
- 1010–970 BC: David reigns as king over the united kingdom of Judah and Israel (kingdom united in 1003).

Less than four hundred years after David's death, the Israelites as a nation lived in exile again, broken and hopeless. Many of their families lay slain in the burned ruins of Jerusalem. Friends were scattered, their hopes as empty as the blowing sands of Babylon. They needed a way out of exile and the restoration of a right spirit before God.

In twenty-five hundred years since that Israelite exile, history has changed dramatically. Their nomadic lives are virtually incomprehensible to us today. Yet for all the seismic shifts of history, the human heart has changed little. Many of us still live in exile, longing like David, and later like the exiles in Babylon, for a clean heart and restoration to the presence of God.

CHAPTER 2

Forgiveness in Fetters

Reading: 2 Chronicles 6

I often wonder if others have a problem with housekeeping. Cleaning, rather. I'm not generally neglectful. I cut the grass every week—a necessity in Michigan—shovel the snow, rake the leaves. I paint what sections of the house need painting, and I wash the car when it starts groaning under the weight of dirt. Neatness is probably a virtue; according to my Dutch mother it was very likely the highest virtue. After all, hers was a household where you put on clean underwear to ride to the beach for a picnic. You wouldn't want to be caught dead in dirty underwear.

My home office, however, has its own set of cleaning ethics. No family member would dare come in and move things around. After all, I know where most things are. Once in a while, with advance warning, my wife will enter, arrange the piles of books, and vacuum the carpet. Rarer still, like when I finish a long project, I tackle the room in a spasm of cleanliness. Before she grew up and learned better, I used to pay my younger daughter to take all the books off the shelves and dust both the books and the shelves. How they shined.

For her pay, I took her out for lunch and then let her select whatever trinket she wanted from a jewelry store.

It was in one such spasm of cleaning that I tackled my jammed files and began sorting into piles the papers destined to be shredded, recycled, trashed, or kept. In one file I found a photocopy of one of those beautiful medieval designs of the Christian universe. At the bottom was earth, then ascending choirs of angels—messengers, powers, and the like. At the apex, representing God, was an all-seeing circular eye within a triangle. With a start, I realized that it very much resembled the eye atop the pyramid in the official seal on United States currency.

The irony is delicious. In the Middle Ages the eye represented three facets of God: all-seeing, all-knowing, and all-powerful. Thus the triangle. What does it represent on our currency for modern humanity? Do we bow before the almighty Lord, or this tattered piece of paper? Whom do we ultimately serve?

The questions are significant. They also apply directly to our consideration of approaching God for forgiveness. This was the essential first step for the Israelites whom Ezra and Nehemiah led out of exile. Nothing would work right unless they laid their need before the all-powerful Lord and trusted in him alone. But what kept them from doing this? In the previous chapter we considered David's steps toward forgiveness. How do we translate these into the language of our time? What prevents us from seeking forgiveness? How do we dare the great risk of setting aside that secret life we covet and expose it openly to God? It is unsafe; it is frightening.

As we explore this first step of seeking a right relationship with God by seeking forgiveness, it is helpful to understand just what it is that prevents so many of us from taking the great risk. Let's imagine for a moment that we are physicians examining a spiritual malady, looking for a cure, and finding it in the Great Physician. The basic issue of forgiveness is who we are before God. Most often we think of ourselves, in that position of needing forgiveness, as persons who have committed certain, specific sins. We search our hearts and tabulate the score. We expect to lay the slate before God's mercy and have him wipe it clean. That expectation is entirely correct but also very limited. Forgiveness is not just a matter of toting up our sins like an accountant at tax time. More profoundly, forgiveness involves the very persons we are, persons by nature turned away from God rather than toward him. In the same way, the Israelites being led out of exile had to rediscover themselves as God's people, and not some foreign ruler's. Therefore, if we are in earnest about examining ourselves and seeking forgiveness, we must consider three modern impediments that prevent us from showing God the full score of our need.

PRETTY GOOD PEOPLE

We like to think of ourselves as pretty good people. Most of us are by any social standard. We can point to any of the bulging prison population, let's say, and declare that I've never been convicted of a crime. Therefore, I'm a pretty good person. Or, let's say, I've lived a pretty good life—service for charities and on church boards, regular religious habits, a conscientious giver of funds. If I have not committed a crime, and if I have contributed to the kingdom, then I'm a pretty good person.

And we are. By any social standards we are pretty good persons. What's to forgive then? Good question. And something of a paradox if we believe that Jesus died to give us life, that he alone is the way, the truth, and the life. He alone can impart to us the grace that cleanses us from sin and transforms us to life.

This matter of grace and forgiveness, then, is a matter of God's standard, not social standards. What exactly is this grace?

Scott Hoezee, in *The Riddle of Grace,* supplies one of the best definitions I have come across: "Grace is that power and gift of God by which he lays our sin on Jesus but then also lays Jesus' righteousness on us such that when God looks at us, he sees only Christ" (27). Thereby, we understand that according to God's spiritual standard there is only one way to goodness— that is, through Jesus. In fact, this way is accessible to all people—to any one of those persons bulging the bars of prisons, to the downtrodden social outcasts wandering city streets, to the person stricken by soul-numbing depression and feeling of no worth to anyone, least of all to God. In *Rumors of Another World,* Philip Yancey observes that "grace means that no mistake we make in life disqualifies us from God's love. It means that no person is beyond redemption, no human stain beyond cleansing" (222). All are equal in need; all are equal before God; all are equal in the miracle of grace.

In fact, our spiritual record reveals that we are not pretty good people at all. Few struggled more powerfully and thoughtfully with this issue than St. Augustine. The starting point for Augustine was one's relation to a Supreme Being: "The fault of an evil begins when one falls from Supreme Being to some being which is less than absolute" (*City of God,* 254). This is precisely what happened in Eden; the fall was nothing more nor less than Adam and Eve turning their eyes from the Supreme Being to something less than absolute— indeed, something forbidden for that very reason.

We must admit that most of our contemporaries merely laugh at the idea of the fall. An old myth, they say, by which one tries to account for an evil that can't be understood anyway. It's much more sensible to believe that the world is random, where bad things happen for no apparent reason.

But God won't have it that way. Read carefully Augustine's explanation of the fall, for it has been a central point of Christian doctrine ever since: "God, the Author of all natures but not of their defects, created man good; but man, corrupt by choice and condemned by justice, has produced a progeny that is both corrupt and condemned" (278–79). Here Augustine echoes the familiar words of Galatians 5:17: "For the sinful nature desires what is contrary to the Spirit, and the Spirit what is contrary to the sinful nature." Wrong, then, is not the consequence of a random universe beset by bad things; it is sin, when our human desires come into conflict with the will of God. So it was in Eden; so it is today. "Thus," writes Augustine, "from a bad use of free choice, a sequence of misfortunes conducts the whole human race" (279).

We prize those moments when all seems well with the world and we are at peace with it. The problem is that we know full well that all is not well in this world and that peace can be as fragile as fine china. More often than not, our personal lives are deeply distressed by temptation, by disorder, and by tragedy. "Evil," writes Cornelius Plantinga, Jr., in *Engaging God's World*, "is what's wrong with the world, and it includes trouble in nature as well as in human nature" (51). In short, our lives on this earth are corrupted. That doesn't mean that we're incapable of doing any good, but that even our best efforts, apart from grace, are marred.

Where does that understanding leave us then? First, we may indeed consider ourselves pretty good people. We are decent. We refrain from horrible actions. We may even actively fight to prevent such actions in society. But, second, we understand that a "pretty good person" is a social definition—just that, nothing less and nothing more. Because, third, we recognize that we are all spiritual persons, affected by the fall, incapable in and of ourselves to choose wisely and willfully

God's will, and all too prone to personal temptation that separates us from God's will. In short, we need forgiveness. We
need grace. We need a redeemer.

THE VICTIM MENTALITY

If our sense of being a pretty good person is one impediment
to forgiveness, a second is the modern victim mentality. This
mind-set started already in Eden with a deft shifting of
blame back and forth. Nonetheless, in our day of litigation
frenzy, victimization has become rooted in our psyches like
never before. It has gone from "she made me do it" to "I
couldn't possibly have done it *but* for her."

The victim mentality sees oneself as essentially good but
wronged by another person. That wrong may have led me to
do wrong, but in a sense it is not my own doing. The person
or condition of which I am the victim forces the wrong. Now,
if I refuse to acknowledge any culpability for the wrong act,
but claim victimization instead, then there can be no forgiveness either. There's nothing to forgive.

Fundamentally, the victim mentality displays an adult
version of a childhood mind-set, excusing our behavior by
pointing to someone else as the cause. For example, our
neighborhood had a "posse" of young boys, including my
younger son, and one girl who had a great outside jump shot.
They were varied in ethnicity and religion. For the most part
they had great times, usually focused around the basketball
hoop in our driveway or the playground at the church up the
street. But, such being the nature of boys, two of them had a
rollicking good fight one evening. I mean broken glasses,
ripped shirts, and such before they were separated. A short
time later the parents brought the battered and much subdued warriors together to shake hands and make peace. But

after they did so, one of the boys turned to the other, pointed at him, and said, "And you! There's going to be some serious suing going on."

It is an ironic mirror to the litigiousness of our age. We all seem to be victims of something and responsible for nothing. It has saturated our society like a gray wet fog bank in which personal accountability hovers at arm's length, seldom seen. The most common response of allegedly guilty parties in our highest courts is no longer to plead the Fifth Amendment but to utter the more cursory, "I don't remember."

Essentially, the victim mentality is not about forgiveness at all but rather about power. The thinking goes like this: If someone/thing influenced me to an action, that person or thing exercised power over me and robbed me of my own power—and consequently my freedom to choose. Certainly, we acknowledge that all kinds of legitimate instances of victimization exist. But sometimes the victim mentality keeps us from confronting ourselves, admitting our wrongs, and seeking forgiveness.

While the victim mentality provides a dishonest assessment of who we are and what we need, and thereby stands in the way of forgiveness, genuine repentance consists of the recognition and admission of what we have done wrong. To receive grace, we have to name our sin.

Consider again the case with King David. We are told in 2 Samuel 11:1 that it was "the time when kings go off to war." But not David. Instead he sent out Joab with the troops while he roamed his palace. And in that roaming he happened to glance over at a nearby rooftop where Bathsheba was taking a bath. Really, all David had to do was turn his head. Did he know that following his desires would sear his life forever? Stunned as he was by the beautiful woman, his passion easily overrode rationality. It usually does.

Like a computer virus, sin has a way of exponentially multiplying itself in a web of lies. David told himself he was a victim of Bathsheba's beauty. So he brought her to the palace, slept with her, and impregnated her. The problem, of course, is that Bathsheba was married. Very well, now David was so deep into the web that he had Uriah killed. Problem solved.

There stands, of course, a Great King above David, one whose standards are inviolable and inflexible. While David acted according to what he *felt*, God acts according to what is *right*. Adultery and murder are not right, so God sent his prophet Nathan to point out this truth to the thick-headed, self-serving David. Nathan does it in a subtle way, using a parable that first kindles David's wrath against the wrong done. Then the shocker falls. Nathan turns to David, levels him with his eyes, and states the truth: "You are the man" (2 Sam. 12:7).

Every sin has consequences. Nathan lists those to be held against David's account. One of the most important ones reads, "Now, therefore, the sword will never depart from your house" (v. 10). We remember that Jesus was of the house (lineage) of David, and fulfilled this prophecy with the sword in his side. Finally, having been faced with the undeniable reality of his wrongdoing from God's prophet, David breaks down and confesses: "I have sinned against the LORD" (v. 13).

Those few words are packed. They represent the exact opposite of the victim mentality. Who has sinned? *I* have. And what have I done? I have *sinned*. And while your sin affects many lives around you, against whom have you sinned first and foremost? I have sinned against the *Lord*.

While the sense that we are pretty good people and the victim mentality are two impediments to self-confrontation, a third, which may be called "generic grace," is no less harmful.

GENERIC GRACE

The very act of seeking forgiveness requires two things. It requests *pardon* for a sin committed and *freedom from* that sin committed. They may seem at first glance to be identical, but consider that pardon focuses upon the *act* while freedom focuses upon the *doer* of the act. Both, however, require the action of grace for forgiveness to be effective. Only through pardon can a person be freed from bondage to that sin.

At this very point, a most important word in Christian theology enters—*repentance.* It is certainly true in our own lives that we, for our own spiritual healing, often have to forgive other people who are unrepentant. They may, in fact, not care at all about the wrongs they have done to us. In *Forgive and Forget,* Lewis Smedes writes: "When someone hurts us meanly, we want him to suffer too. We expect this clod to pay his dues, we want him to grovel a little. The old-fashioned word for what we want is *repentance"* (89). Smedes goes on to point out that many people use apologies rather than genuine repentance. Apology is the life of generic grace, repentance is the life of spiritual grace. If that is so, however, it again raises the problem of confrontation. What was the act committed? Do I accept responsibility for that act? Often we try a spiritual short-circuit around both and go directly for the grace. It's doomed to failure.

A parallel appears here for those of us who are dealing with the habitual sins of others. I'm thinking, for example, of the hard situation of wayward, prodigal children. Their lifestyles might offend us in every way possible, but we also recognize that they are an offense to the Lord. Do we stand idly by? Do we go to the altar and pray that God will turn them around? Surely we do the latter, often on our knees with tears and aching hearts. But we bear the responsibility of also confronting their wrong. I like the way Nancy Pearcey put it in her book on worldviews, *Total Truth:*

> Putting our valid needs on the altar does not mean shutting our mouths and closing our eyes to a sinful situation. If someone is truly in the wrong, then the loving response is not to give in but to confront the person. It is not an act of love to allow someone to sin against you with impunity. Sin is a cancer within the other person's soul, and genuine love must be strong and courageous in bringing that sin to light, where it can be diagnosed and dealt with. (357)

We ourselves cannot heal our children's spiritual cancer. We simply bear two responsibilities as Christian parents: to pray for them and to point out to them the waywardness of their lives from God's will.

A gap like a chasm exists between seeking forgiveness for a very specific act, one we name and seek both pardon for and freedom from, and a kind of request for generic grace that soothes us without any of the pain of specification. Generic grace represents the fear of confronting a specific need for forgiveness and manifests itself simply as a general prayer for forgiveness. It is as random and unstructured as a cell phone conversation while driving. The old song "I Love to Tell the Story" has the refrain, "For our sins he suffered! For our sins he died!" Yes, indeed. That is the foundation of our faith. The crucifixion and resurrection reign as the centering points of Christianity. But for *what* sins did Jesus die to pardon us in the crucifixion, and from *what* sins did he free us in the resurrection?

If generic grace is an impediment to genuine, life-transforming forgiveness, what constitutes genuine grace? First, recognize that generic grace doesn't cost anything. In *The Cost of Discipleship*, very likely one of the most important religious books of the twentieth century, Dietrich Bonhoeffer made it altogether clear that generic grace is "cheap grace." He knew by experience the cost of genuine grace, having stood up for his Christian principles in Nazi Germany until he was executed in a concentration camp. Bonhoeffer wrote that "cheap grace is grace without discipleship, grace without the cross, grace without Jesus Christ, living and incarnate" (45).

Each of those three "withouts" bears emphasis, for each cheapens grace. First, cheap grace is without discipleship. This means that it is without pattern or principle. It does not operate out of obedience to any higher authority in our lives. Cheap grace is a matter of convenience.

Second, cheap grace is without the cross. It does not find a meaningful purpose for forgiveness, but instead is simply relative to our wishes. Ezra gives an interesting historical twist on this matter of forgiveness. After opposition started against his rebuilding of the altar in Jerusalem, a letter was sent to King Darius to search the royal archives for an earlier decree by King Cyrus. When discovered, the decree provided full financial support for rebuilding. Most important, however, is the concluding sentence: "Furthermore, I decree that if anyone changes this edict, a beam is to be pulled from his house and he is to be lifted up and impaled on it. And for this crime his house is to be made a pile of rubble" (Ezra 6:11). In this case, one man who was guilty of violating the authority of an earthly king was impaled upon a cross.

We know that all things in the Old Testament point toward their fulfillment in the New Testament. Jesus told Nicodemus, "Just as Moses lifted up the snake in the desert, so the Son of Man must be lifted up, that everyone who believes in him may have eternal life" (John 3:14–15). King Cyrus assigned death on the cross for the criminal. Moses lifted up the snake as a symbol of deliverance for the sins of the Israelites. Jesus fulfilled both of these symbols when he died for the crimes of others for deliverence from sin.

Which brings us directly to Bonhoeffer's third point, for neither of the first two makes any sense unless we believe in "Jesus Christ, living and incarnate." That's the bottom line. If Jesus were not the incarnate Son of God, as he claimed to be, then his death on the cross would be that of just another rabble-rouser. If that is all the cross represents, we might just as well, like Moses, stick up poles of snakes on our walls and church steeples. Jesus is the Son of God, sinless, incarnate, who alone could take on our guilt when he endured the cross. This was not "cheap grace"; it cost the blood of the Son of God.

Sometimes we get so comfortable with our understanding of the Bible that we wear it like a favorite old sweatshirt. This is especially so when we think of the cross and the work Jesus did there. Our general concept is that the cross is all about love. While that's the subject of countless Christian songs and sermons, it's only partially true. God's great and mysterious love for us *motivated* the cross. That love we'll never fully comprehend on this side of heaven. But we receive enough glimpses of it to know it is true. The cross is the central glimpse, when heaven cracked open and God said, "This is true love."

But the cross, Jesus' dying there in agony, that *act* itself and not the motivation, is all about justice. Humanity violated holiness. When David sinned with Bathsheba, a debt had to be paid. His firstborn child, the one he had impregnated her with during their adulterous liaison, died shortly after birth. That was the penalty for David's sin. But justice for all humanity? Balancing the scales for my sin so that I can come clean before the holiness of God? This took not a firstborn child, but the only begotten Son of God. Only someone eternally and intrinsically holy could satisfy this justice with such expensive grace on the cross.

When we have the three—a pretty good person, the victim mentality, and generic grace—working together, we are, as a friend of mine from southeastern Ohio used to put it, "in a heap of trouble deeper than a cornfield." It can be pretty hard to find your way around in a late summer cornfield. Looking at the spiritual alternatives to these three—fallen humanity, personal responsibility, and genuine grace—we feel a certain desperation to find a way out of the maze.

We seldom like to confront those well-layered inner lives we carry around. If we continue to deny the need for confrontation, we fail to find true pardon and freedom, and thereby more layers accumulate around that needy inner self. If pardon and freedom are the genuine touchstones of our Christian faith, we are also missing out on the genuine spiritual glory of our faith. Working through the steps of confrontation—meeting our need and finding God's answer—will lead to a far happier ending than we dared imagine. That ending is restoration to a living relationship with God, something that constantly eludes the victim mentality or the seeker of generic grace. We want nothing less than to rebuild our spiritual walls to locate a sure, sacred place where we can know God.

How do these brief passages in the Old Testament help us in that work? It is a curious thing that the Lord who led Israel out of bondage in Egypt now allowed them to be led into bondage in Persia. Why? To understand this also requires an act of confrontation. By examining that event in the Israelites' life, we can go a long way toward understanding ourselves in our present spiritual events.

CHAPTER 3

The Captive Nation

Reading: 2 Chronicles 35:15—Ezra 1:7

In the previous chapter we considered three ways by which we avoid confronting the reality of our sins—the belief that we are pretty good persons, the victim mentality, and generic grace. Like settling into a high-powered car and going in reverse, these are means of turning away from God in a hurry. In Psalm 139 David asks, "Where can I go from your Spirit? Where can I flee from your presence?" (7). But as David realized, one can't flee. He took it as an enormous comfort. For some of us the thought is so haunting we wish God would leave us alone. Whatever the case, the true nature of our need and answers for that need won't appear until we visit the ophthalmologist's office, for we need a whole new way of seeing. We need, if you will, corrected vision. Consider an example from the Soviet prison camps of the past century.

We probably imagine an *archipelago* as a body of water with a string, or "arch," of many small islands. We imagine them as emerald green clusters rising from the waters of the South Pacific. Light breezes drift across sugar-sand beaches. A dream vacation takes shape in our minds.

For many years in the Soviet Union the term had an entirely different meaning. This archipelago was a string of prison camps extending across the frozen wastes of Siberia. The camp prisoners were forced to work building canals, railroads, and roads. Many died from the bitter weather and malnutrition. Even in the ice-locked regions of Siberia, their sleeping quarters were simple wooden barracks and their diet seldom more than bread and water or porridge. Many collapsed at their labor, their bodies as well as their minds simply exhausted. And many of those who had the audacity to speak out were executed as incorrigibles.

What did the state do with the thousands of corpses during the harsh Siberian winters? The frozen ground couldn't be broken for burial. They stacked them up like cordwood until the spring thaws. Then many of them were crushed into the concrete that lined the Trans-Caucasus Canal.

Such experiences inscribe their horror upon a person's soul. For some it was a story that had to be told or one's soul would die. For Aleksandr Solzhenitsyn, telling the story became his reason for living, for he too had been a prisoner of those camps. His own arrest, as it nearly always did, came by surprise. As a captain in the Soviet army, he was ordered to see his commanding officer. Upon arriving there, he found members of the secret police who accused him of being a traitor. The evidence? A letter he had written to a friend in which he had criticized some official. From there, the events took a nearly ludicrous turn. Solzhenitsyn's captors got lost on the trip to the prison and had to ask the military captain to read the maps that would lead them there. Then the doors of the Gulag Archipelago slammed shut. For eleven years Solzhenitsyn endured it and lived to tell its true story.

When he did, when the first pieces leaked out to the Western press, and when eventually the Cold War began to thaw, then a curious thing happened. Many of Solzhenitsyn's own people shrank from the story. "Oh, don't tell," they said. "It is far too awful. It must be forgotten now." Then, as Solzhenitsyn reports it, "Those same hands which once screwed tight our handcuffs now hold up their palms in reconciliation: 'No, don't! Don't dig up the past! Dwell on the past and you lose an eye.'"

But Solzhenitsyn reminds them that the Russian proverb they cite goes on to say, "Forget the past and you lose both eyes."

Many Christians today are crippled in sin-worlds without means of confession and healing. As Solzhenitsyn urges, we are compelled to remember, and by doing so become liberated. The difficulty today is that, like Solzhenitsyn's protestors, we don't even see the need. We find it hard to talk about sin— not sin in general, but *my* sin. It seems spiritually impolite among Christians to do so. We shy away from confession like we would try to avoid a head-on collision with a semi. Sometimes the best we do is a "moment of silence" intended to name our sins during a corporate prayer of confession.

Yet something in us, called a conscience, longs to be free from captivity to sin. We want to strip away the walls of being a pretty good person, of victim mentality, and of generic grace. We sense that if only we could escape those walls of sin-imprisonment, we could begin to rebuild the foundations of a new life where we can have a fresh taste of joy.

Solzhenitsyn's proverb begins to chart a course for us. As he insisted, we too live with one eye on the spiritual and personal traditions that have shaped us. We also see how we have acted within that tradition, what our responsibilities and wrongdoings have been. As 1 John 2:11 puts it, sometimes we feel blinded by the dark. It is the dark imprisonment of our own wrongdoings. With the other eye, we want to look to the future. We have hopes and anticipations, plans and obligations. As well, we may have fears and conflicts that so overwhelm us that we awaken each morning with a cold, choking dread. Where we stand at the present may seem a very confusing place.

With my utmost respect for Aleksandr Solzhenitsyn, a powerful Christian voice crying in the wilderness of the communistic and atheistic Soviet Union, his message at the time was primarily historical and political. He wanted to bring to light what was hidden in history so that it wouldn't be repeated. But we need more than that. We need a spiritual accounting to keep our feet from sliding into our own desert places.

THE ROOT OF THE PROBLEM

The second book of Chronicles compresses history into a mind-numbing litany of sin. With the notable exception of the last great reformer, King Josiah (639–609 BC), the spiritual lives of the Israelites were evaporating faster than ice chips on a hot griddle. Soon nothing was left but empty air and the heat of their own passions. Chronicles ends by reminding us of the guilt of the people, for which God allowed them to be led into Babylon. It is almost as if God was saying, "See—this is what you have done; this is the consequence."

The peculiar tragedy of what the people did is that it didn't have to be that way. The pattern of the Chronicles is not simply a historical record of kings and people; it is a testament of how God reaches into human history to try to draw his beloved people to himself. In 2 Chronicles 7:14 God testifies, "If my people, who are called by my name, will humble themselves and pray and seek my face and turn from their wicked ways, then will I hear from heaven and will forgive their sin and will heal their land." This is a powerful example of "conditions and promises."

The people were to pray and seek God's face. In their surrounding polytheistic culture, the Israelites sought help everywhere *but* from God. They sought it in magic, in idols, in signs and omens. They replaced worship of the living God with the death-bringing things of evil. The difficulty with wandering away from God's plan is that each step *seems* to get easier rather than harder. It is a strange but accurate psychology—no less true today. Yet in the end, it's more difficult. Tempted into one sin, one has to lie to cover it up, and the accumulation of falsehoods grows into a mountain we can neither carry nor undo in our own strength.

So too, when the Israelites turned from God's will to seeking their own immediate answers, it became ever easier to walk into wicked ways. God became a distant whisper, an annoying echo of some past that barely registered in their minds. Thus, God called to them, "Turn from your wicked ways."

Even so, God holds out hope to us just as he did with the Israelites. Why? Because of his great love that we are not consumed (see Lam. 3:32). Therefore God promises very specific responses to the necessary conditions: I will hear; I will forgive; I will heal. The most amazing thing is that the Israelites didn't much care about humbling themselves, seeking God, and turning from their wicked ways. God kept reaching out. The Israelites kept pushing his hand away. They needed a tremendous wake-up call. It came with the Babylonian army.

God alone knows what "Babylonian army" he has stored for us on the horizon today, but it is necessary to have this brief overview of the entrance into exile as a lesson of hope to guide us. However dismal the deeds of humanity may seem at times, the God of glory holds out a shining hope. Remember that as we consider some of the following challenges. We want to look at the wrong to see how God can make it right. We want to see the darkness that hides joy to understand God's bright righteousness that brings joy. We want to feel that breath of glory that comes from God alone, the joy of knowing that whatever we struggle with here on earth, he can transform into good. That is the place where we hope to arrive.

We all have our individual excuses and defense mechanisms. We examined several of these in the prior chapter. Yet these are symptoms of a deeper problem. If you go to your family doctor when you're not feeling well, you list those items that don't feel normal—a headache, fever, dizziness. Considering your symptoms, the doctor makes a diagnosis, anything from fatigue to West Nile virus, and prescribes a course of treatment. In the same way, our reliance upon such escape mechanisms—escape from confronting our need—as pretty good people, the victim mentality, and generic grace are symptoms of a more serious, core problem.

In the Middle Ages, those people with a religious sensibility had a hierarchy of the seven deadly sins. It wasn't just a list, but also a structure of human nature starting at the bottom with bodily wrongs, then to attitudes, then to the intellectual sins. Thus, lust was at the bottom because it was an action of bodily passion. Sloth was a character disorder, but not particularly harmful to anyone else. Anger, on the other hand, was near the top because it nearly always involves someone else. In fact, it can lead a person to attack and revile one's neighbor. Envy is yet more serious because it's a two-way disorder—dissatisfaction with one's own state and desiring another's. Its effects may ensue in theft, destruction, even murder.

But at the very top of this hierarchy of sin lies pride. In *Not the Way It's Supposed to Be: A Breviary of Sin,* Cornelius

Plantinga, Jr., wittily describes pride: "People still have affairs with themselves" (82). Considered carefully, that's about as good a definition of pride as one could get, for in pride all relations revolve around and are secondary to the I. Plantinga goes on to describe the effects of pride:

> In an ego-centered culture, wants become needs (maybe even duties), the self replaces the soul, and human life degenerates into the clamor of competing autobiographies. People get fascinated with how they feel—and how they feel about how they feel. In such a culture and in the throes of such fascination, the self exists to be explored, indulged, and expressed but not disciplined or restrained. (83)

And what happens to God? Well, God too then, and necessarily, becomes secondary to self. Examples of such pride permeate the Chronicles like a long, slow stream of toxic sludge. In fact, even some of the apparently good kings let the crown of kingship go to their heads.

Second Chronicles 26 tells the story of King Uzziah, who assumed the throne at age sixteen and reigned fifty-one years (792–740 BC). In his early years he was fortunate to have the mentorship of the prophet Zechariah. What's more, Uzziah listened to him. And "as long as he sought the LORD, God gave him success" (v. 5). He drove out Philistines, rebuilt towns and portions of Jerusalem, and outfitted an army of more than 300,000 men. As 2 Chronicles notes, "His fame spread far and wide, for he was greatly helped until he became powerful" (v. 15).

Did you catch the hitch in that verse? *Until* he became powerful. What happened then? We find out in the next verse: "But after Uzziah became powerful, his pride led to his downfall" (v. 16).

Here's the pure audacity of his pride. Unfaithful to God now, and reliant upon himself, he swaggered into the temple of God to burn incense on the altar. This, of course, was a sacred altar, attended only by Azariah the chief priest. With eighty "courageous" priests following him, Azariah confronted the king: "It is not right for you, Uzziah, to burn incense to the LORD. That is for the priests, the descendants of Aaron, who have been consecrated to burn incense. Leave the sanctuary, for you have been unfaithful; and you will not be honored by the LORD God" (v. 18). Uzziah lashed out in anger; his pride was insulted. One can almost read his raging mind: "I am the powerful king!" Then a patch of leprosy broke out on his forehead. And spread. He lived as an outcast until the day he died.

But Uzziah was an outcast long before leprosy afflicted him. It began with that first taste of power and pride that grew inside him like an internal leprosy. The external disease was merely the symptom of the internal disorder.

A RENEWED VISION

I am reminded of another king in 2 Chronicles. Jehoshaphat couldn't have been in more nerve-wracking and energy-sapping straits. The vast Moabite army had Jehoshaphat's land cordoned off. One would think his mind would be scurrying for a plan of escape. Instead, he proclaims a fast and then prays. Interesting—he prepares himself by fasting and then prays. This is no desperation prayer targeted like an arrow at God's mercy. Generic grace won't do here. Jehoshaphat concludes his prayer with these words: "We have no power to face this vast army that is attacking us. We do not know what to do, but our eyes are upon you" (20:12). Perhaps you know the rest of the story. The people go singing (!) into battle, for they know

that "the battle is not yours, but God's" (v. 15). Here is the consequence. As the Israelite army marches out, the singers shout
out, "Give thanks to the Lord, for his love endures forever" (v.
21). At that very moment, "The Lord set ambushes" that
ensnared the enemy forces. They began fighting each other. By
the time the Israelite army arrived, "They saw only dead bodies lying on the ground; no one had escaped" (v. 24). They
would not have known that victory, however, and they would
not have had the heart to go singing into battle, had they not
seized that quiet, intimate moment before the battle and
turned their eyes upon the Lord.

Turning their eyes *from* God was the first step in spiritual
dying for the Israelites. Each person did what was right in his
own eyes, and veiled his eyes toward God. A grim lesson
emerges. The first surefire step in spiritual dying is to turn our
gaze from God to our own harried lives: ignoring personal
spiritual time with God. Forget about the Bible gathering dust
on the shelf. Let prayer dwindle to quick shotgun messages
fired into the air.

The remedy begins with the act of restoration—making
that quiet time of devotional intimacy, reading God's Word,
and listening for his voice in prayer. When one kneels in
prayer, it has been said, one kneels on the neck of Satan.

The second book of Chronicles almost seems to pain the
writer, so faithful in his history to this point. In 2 Chronicles
36:15 he writes, "The LORD, the God of their fathers, sent
word to them through his messengers again and again,
because he had pity on his people and on his dwelling
place." I find it hard to imagine such compassion. God
reached out to his people, calling them to his sacred place for
restoration. But what was their reaction? "They mocked
God's messengers, despised his words and scoffed at his
prophets until the wrath of the Lord was aroused against his

people and there was no remedy" (v. 16). What a fearful thing it is to stand in the wrath of the Lord, rather than in the warm embrace of his compassion!

In the year 586 BC, the Babylonian king Nebuchadnezzar, who had formerly captured the northern kingdom of Israel in 605 BC, now marched on Judah and its capital city, Jerusalem. The city held out against the Babylonian siege for almost two years, but when the end came, it came with devastating thoroughness. Since the Israelites had made the sacred temple a hollow shell, Nebuchadnezzar simply finished the deed physically. He slaughtered everyone huddled in the temple for sanctuary. He carried off all the treasures, set fire to the building, and tore down the wall of Jerusalem as a parting gesture. The city was gutted. As the people were led away into captivity, there lay only a mournful vacancy behind them, a home for jackals and night creatures.

During Cyrus's reign the most dramatic changes began to take place. He was a Persian king. When he defeated the Babylonians in 539 BC, he paved the way for the exiles' return. It also, not incidentally, fulfilled Jeremiah's prophecy of a seventy-year Babylonian captivity (see Jer. 25:11–12; 29:10).

Most likely, from his own point of view Cyrus was simply being pragmatic in his decision to permit the return of the Israelites. His primary allegiance was to the god Marduk. We find none of the talk that usually accompanies a God-sent vision or command. Here he was, the new ruler of an empire, with a number of different nationalities living in the land. Meanwhile, there was the problem of governing these far-flung territories under his rule. Now, what would be better? To have his garrisons of troops draining the national treasury by living in those foreign lands, or to let the natives find their way back to those lands, rebuild their homes, work the land, and eventually pay him an annual tribute? This is the likeliest scenario for Cyrus's proclamation in Ezra 1:2 that "the Lord, the God of heaven" had led him to permit an Israelite return to Jerusalem. Ezra testifies, in effect, that God will work however and through whomever he wills.

Cyrus permitted the Jews to collect a freewill offering to finance the return of the first group. More important, he dug into Nebuchadnezzar's horde of riches and found the sacred vessels of the temple. He turned these over to the returning exiles as well.

What a remarkable moment in history. What the world meant for evil, God turned to good. Out of the battles that raged across the Middle East, God raised a man, who had no particular knowledge of God, to do his express will. If one despot cast the Israelites in chains, another loosed those chains.

Often we look as the Israelites did—scanning the situation around us for signs of our salvation. We won't find them in the world of humanity, for this is a sin-closed world, a world over which extends, as C. S. Lewis put it, "that hideous strength" of Satan. Yet at our very moment of desolation, God can rip into this world to execute his will in *his* way. Consider these words in Psalm 107:12–14. Because of the people's rebellion, the psalmist writes,

> [God] subjected them to bitter labor;
>   they stumbled, and there was no one to help.
> Then they cried to the LORD in their trouble,
>   and he saved them from their distress.
> He brought them out of darkness and the deepest
>   gloom and broke away their chains.

God is not captive in history; he is the Lord of history. We live in linear cause and effect, planning our actions so that they will arrive at the precise endpoint *we* want. But God is a Lord of mysteries. The writer of Ecclesiastes tells us, "As you do not know the path of the wind, or how the body is formed in a mother's womb, so you cannot understand the work of God, the Maker of all things" (11:5). The challenge for us is not necessarily to plan every detail of our lives, but to live with our eyes turned toward God who has a future and a hope (Jer. 29:11) for each of our lives. Thus it is by God's mysterious action that Cyrus made the decision to "break away their chains," and to let the exiles go.

But who would lead them?

Here it gets interesting. Many assume, since they are the prominently named leaders in the return, that Ezra and Nehemiah lead the Israelites back from exile. However, two little-known characters, Sheshbazzar and Zerubbabel, stepped out of the shadows of history to start the great work. So shadowy are their places, in fact, that some scholars have identified them as the same person. The most widely accepted scenario, however, is that Sheshbazzar was an older man who started the work on the temple that Zerubbabel later developed.

We shouldn't let the peculiarities of the *how* deflect us from the *what* that actually happened. In 537 BC, after some four months of traveling across desert and mountains from Babylon to Jerusalem, the first exiles returned. Probably none of them had ever seen the city. Did they feel any quickening in their pulses as they traveled down along the Jordan River toward Jerusalem? Was there any call from the Lord saying that this was home?

Sometimes after a long vacation trip, when you finally point the hood of the car back toward home, you can almost feel a tingling in your whole body. I well remember traveling from Pennsylvania with our three little children at the time packed into the old Chevy to visit our parents in Michigan. During the last miles as we approached one of their homes, the children would fall silent with anticipation. It was still strange to them—to be this far from their own home. But when we returned to Pennsylvania, they knew every land-mark. How the hills became steeper just past Youngstown. When we turned off the highway onto the two-lane road, they saw the dairy where we bought our milk in glass bottles. There was the barn where our church had square dances and the kids played hide and seek in the cornfield. Then the last turn, where they could see our big old yellow house, and they all leaned forward with anticipation.

But what did the Israelites see?

A land of broken walls and scattered rubble. The homes were looted, burned, and littered. Animals from the sur-rounding hills skittered down the streets or slunk to their dens in collapsed houses. And the temple lay flattened and desolate as if hit by an earthquake.

This is home?

CHAPTER 4

At God's Altar

Reading: Ezra 3:1–6

In its earliest use in the Old Testament, the meeting between God and human was the foundational concept of the altar. But humans in their own nature were unworthy to meet God. That face-to-face communion ended when sin besmirched Eden. Therefore, an atoning sacrifice was offered on the altar as a sign of humans wanting to be right with God. The Hebrew word for *altar* literally means "place of sacrifice."

During the age of the Patriarchs, there was no such thing as a priesthood, the anointed intercessors between humans and God. Yet the Patriarchs did build their own altars, and they did hold sacrifices upon them to commemorate some special event of God in the lives of his people. For example, Noah built an altar after the flood. In response, God covenanted his blessings (see Gen. 8:21—9:17). Abraham built several altars for sacrifice, including the one at Moriah where he was to offer Isaac but God supplied a ram instead (see Gen. 22:12–14). Isaac, Jacob, and Moses all erected altars.

The design of the altar was first given by God to Moses. Specifically, it was to be crafted from earth or unhewn rock (see Ex. 20:24–26). These are the most basic elements of God's creation. In fact, God tells Moses that the altar will be defiled if anyone uses tools on the rocks. At this time, then, the altar took on a central role in Jewish life and worship. When Solomon built his temple, the altar then became the featured point of the house of the Lord. If things were wrong, here you could make them right with God.

For the Israelites returning from exile, the altar represented several things. It was, above all, a declaration. We will freely and bravely worship the Lord *our* God. They had been surrounded by a host of altars and a confusing array of gods in polytheistic Babylon. Freedom lay in the declaration that they were God's people now.

Furthermore, the altar represented their unity as a nation. That nation was small and dangerously weak at this moment in history. They had left exile under one of the most powerful rulers the Middle East had ever known. His word was absolute and could bring sudden, violent death. But God worked in him to release the captives, who were free now to unify their nation under God, their true Deliverer.

A third significance of the altar was to atone for transgressions. The burnt offering—an unblemished bull, for example—constituted a shedding of blood "because of the uncleanness and rebellion of the Israelites, whatever their sins have been" (Lev. 16:16). The goat had a special function as "scapegoat." The priest would lay his hands on the goat's head, confess the sins of the Israelites, thus transferring them to the goat, and drive the goat into the wilderness. Thereby the priestly ceremony of the altar both atoned for human sins and also carried them far away into the wilderness. The symbolic act lay behind David's words about God in Psalm 103:11–12:

> For as high as the heavens are above the earth, so
> great is his love for those who fear him; as far
> as the east is from the west, so far has he
> removed our transgressions from us.

The altar of sacrifice, then, was a means of moving into God's loving grace.

Finally, the altar represented an offering of people's lives and prayers to God. With the establishment of the priesthood through Aaron, the offering of incense began. "Aaron must burn fragrant incense" (Ex. 30:7). It was a costly offering (one of which was frankincense) and represented the people's lives before God. In Psalm 141:2 David made it clear that prayers were like a fragrant offering to God:

> May my prayer be set before you like incense;
> may the lifting up of my hands be like the
> evening sacrifice.

In all these cases, the altar was the centering stage where God's people came into his presence.

Most Christian churches still maintain an altar, either of wood or stone. The altar is both a place of remembrance and also a symbol of Christ's perfect fulfillment. Often it is the place from which the Lord's Supper is served. This too is the place where God's people gather as a new people, drawn out of exile "from every nation, tribe, people, and language" (Rev. 7:9). Here we remember that our sins are atoned for by the perfect sacrifice, "a lamb without blemish or defect" (1 Peter 1:19). Here too we bring our prayers and our praises as an offering to our Redeemer: "Through Jesus, therefore, let us continually offer to God a sacrifice of praise—the fruit of lips that confess his name" (Heb. 13:15).

Paul wrote to the Ephesians: "Be imitators of God,

therefore, as dearly loved children and live a life of love, just as Christ loved us and gave himself up for us as a fragrant offering and sacrifice to God" (5:1–2).

Two implications arise from this passage that exhort us to be imitators of Christ and to make our lives a fragrant offering to him. First, we ourselves are that temple where offerings are made. This theme beats like lifeblood behind Paul's other teachings. Thus in 1 Corinthians 3:16, "Don't you know that you yourselves are God's temple and that God's Spirit lives in you?" Variations of the verse appear in many other passages, but the implication in each is clear—our very lives constitute God's temple. This temple needs every bit of the same care the Israelites afforded theirs. It needs the fragrance of a sweet offering within, but as we discover through Nehemiah, it also needs strong protection from without.

A second implication arises from this concept that we ourselves are the temple of God. The temple was and continues to be a place where others come to be ministered to, renewed, and illuminated. In 2 Corinthians Paul wrote of the Christian life being a fragrant offering: "For we are to God the aroma of Christ among those who are being saved and those who are perishing" (2:15). Then he changed his metaphor slightly: "You show that you are a letter from Christ, the result of our ministry, written not with ink but with the Spirit of the living God, not on tablets of stone but on tablets of human hearts" (3:3). Never is the task of believers to bottle up the Spirit in their own temples. Offering our lives like incense is only half of the equation. The other half is the question, "Now what do we do with our lives?"

REBUILDING THE ALTAR

Sheshbazzar may have been an elderly man when he arrived in Jerusalem. Possibly he delegated the work to others. All the biblical account tells us is that when the Israelites arrived and began work, it was directed by Jeshua the priest and Zerubbabel the civil authority. Apparently, their greatest concern was just where to begin. Marauding tribes still prowled the land about them. Perhaps the walls should be built first. Dwelling places lay in ruins. The people needed places to live. Perhaps their needs came first. Or how about the temple itself? Isn't that why they came? The temple was merely a memory; the actual building had been leveled.

None of these was the first priority. The first thing then, as it is now, was to build a sacred place where the people could come heart to heart before God. The really remarkable passage in this story lies in that first action: "Despite their fear of the peoples around them, they built the altar on its foundation and sacrificed burnt offerings to the LORD, both the morning and evening sacrifices" (Ezra 3:3). Perhaps spies from Israel's traditional enemies had caught wind of the return by now, peering in from hidden places. How ludicrous it must have appeared to them. This small and largely defenseless band of people cleaned out the altar place, then rebuilt it in the proper manner of their people, laboriously, with unhewn stones. Then they gathered at the site and stared at an offering going up in smoke.

Yet one wonders if these spies felt a strange touch of fear. The scene may appear ludicrous, but the very bravery of this act of faith in the presence of one's enemies is worrisome. What if this very place *is* one where the divine and human meet?

In many respects, we are little different from the Israelites—our elder brothers and sisters in the Lord. It takes an act of infinite courage to cleanse the altar of our hearts, to make our very lives—heart, soul, mind, and strength—a sacred place for God. But it is always the first thing. Before we even think about building our public temples, we had better purify our personal altars.

"But," one might say, "I am really, really afraid to open myself up like this. I will feel so exposed, so ... messy and weak."

That's exactly why we come. None of us is alone in that respect. Paul wrote in Romans 3:23–24, "For all have sinned and fall short of the glory of God, and are justified freely by his grace through the redemption that came by Christ Jesus." The difficulty with the "country-club" church, where we pay the fee of our offerings for membership, is that there appears to be no necessity to challenge people as sinners, thus no need to call them to the altar of forgiveness. The altar, however, always begins in our own hearts. The first act is how we meet Jesus, making room for him and letting his conviction lead us.

Consider also this matter of fear upon coming to the altar. The Israelites feared marauding tribes and their traditional enemies. It took courage to stand there exposed and nearly defenseless and to show by their deeds that this was the God they served. We all have such fears before our own altar where we meet God. We fear that we are not worthy, that the altar will remain vacant and lifeless, that our offering will be scorned.

At the altar you are alone with God, and to him you are of infinite worth. The most amazing thing is that, unlike any other religion in the world, you don't have to earn your worth *before* coming to the altar. In fact, it isn't earned at all. It is freely given by the coming itself. We lay our unworthiness on the altar. That is all we have to offer. We walk away loved and held precious by the Lord who bestows worth freely and without finding fault (see Heb. 4:16; James 1:5).

Fear is not something to be taken lightly. If fears are real to the person holding them, they are serious indeed, and to be taken seriously. This is especially true of spiritual fears, and in the sense of feeling too unworthy to come before God. The Israelites had fears in abundance—marauding armies, discord among their own tribes, instability in ruling powers. But fears are also internal, and so too are ours today. In fact, I find three specific fears holding a powerful grip on Christians today.

THE TYRANNY OF TIME

No other issue—theological, spiritual, or psychological—has been as extensively addressed in contemporary Christendom as this: the cluttered schedules of our time, the irresolvable conflict of demands. Ours is a hurried age.

We are hurried by scores of chores, from school committees to workloads so top heavy they seem like mountains to scale. Our Christian lives are similarly time-warped with demands, from the essentials of devotional and worship time to the obligations of committees that proliferate in the modern church with all the abandon of amoebas in a swamp. The little things collide and grow huge in mass. The waters grow increasingly turgid.

Responsibility is the burden of the modern age. Called to do so many things, we become driven by the things that call us. Enough, we say. We want to see one path clearly, not a myriad of byways leading who knows where.

In his poem "Birches," Robert Frost writes, "It is when I'm weary of considerations/And life is too much like a pathless wood" that he would like to get away from it for a while, maybe swing on a birch tree in the ecstatic freedom of childhood, when one has little to do all day but play at being free and easy. Perhaps all our later lives are a longing for such childhood. The key word in Frost's lines, however, the word under which the freedom of childhood crumbles, is *considerations*. These are the little petty, annoying demands on our time and energy that accumulate into an overwhelming maze, making life itself a pathless wood.

Where does one go when one discovers that the pathless wood is where one stands, uncertain, a bit lost and befuddled, except for the certainty of being overwhelmed?

The priorities of time the world places upon us are one matter, but the spiritual life also has its demands. The first step in combating the tyranny of time is to set spiritual priorities, in this case the discernment of gifts and calling. What makes our schedules so hectic, quite simply, is that so many of us, well intentioned to be sure, are doing things we should not do. Not that they are bad things. Many of them are quite good. Some are simply frivolous. But still not the right thing for a given individual.

The modern church faces a crisis of time management, and it extends from the pastor to all the members. The management of the crisis itself may be resolved by doing first things first—discovering what gifts God has equipped members with for service. God has equipped each member, and has called each member to a task. To Jeremiah the Lord said,

> Before I formed you in the womb I knew you,
>   before you were born I set you apart;
> I appointed you as a prophet to the nations.
>   (Jeremiah 1:5)

Not all of us are appointed prophets, but each of us has been formed by the Lord and consecrated for a task in his kingdom.

The church will never run out of gifted people equipped to do the tasks of the church. It may run out of burned-out members who don't know what their gifts and tasks are. The church and its members face a twofold task: first, inventorying the spiritual gifts of its congregation; second, matching the gifted persons to the right tasks. Add a third: the responsibility of individuals to say no to those tasks not suited to their gifts. The church thereby relies on the wisdom of God and the work of the Holy Spirit to accomplish its tasks.

Clearly this task demands careful education and training. It is not a matter of sitting people down in a circle and selecting from a gross list: This I can or want to do; this I don't. Education consists of defining biblical and personal gifts. Training consists of equipping the person to best utilize these gifts in the church. To stand firm before the tyranny of time, we need to know first who we are; second, what we can do; third, how to do it.

An important qualification applies here. While certain members of the church have gifts to serve the church—as prophets, pastors, teachers, organists, custodians, evangelists, child caretakers—the call to serve in God's kingdom extends to all members. Service lies at the very root of our Christian life.

In "Birches" Frost also carefully noted: "May no fate willfully misunderstand me/And half grant what I wish." Frost recognized that to step aside from the harried pace of life for a time was not to forsake life. Life is "the right place for love," he wrote. We should also point out that the encouragement to individual ministry, to ordering a private life by discovering and using individual gifts, is similarly not an escape from life. Rather, such gift discovery and spiritual ordering enable one to engage life from the certitude of having a place to stand. Knowing who we are, and what God has called us to do, provides the basis for a *joyful* engagement of life, a sense of victorious labor rather than servile drudgery.

The first threat to one's developing faith, then, is simply the tyranny of time in this modern world. And the way to counter the threat, to protect the foundation, is to discover one's gifts for service in God's kingdom. That kingdom is precisely this time-tyrannized life we live in. In his study *Celebration of Discipline,* Richard Foster remarks that "the Disciplines are best experienced in the midst of our normal daily activities. If they are to have any transforming effect, the effect must be found in the ordinary junctures of human life: in our relationships with our husband or wife, our brothers and sisters, our friends and neighbors" (131). In this sense, the discovery of spiritual gifts is an inward action to enable an outward activity—service in God's kingdom. All gifts, all ministries, are not for ourselves but for engagement of the world where our faith takes root and bears fruit.

In Thomas Kelly's posthumously published *A Testament of Devotion,* there appears one of those brief, beautiful passages that sparkle like a gem. He speaks to our experience of time and how God's voice breaks into it from all eternity: "Deep within us all there is an amazing inner sanctuary of the soul, a holy place, a Divine Center, a speaking Voice, to which we may continuously return. Eternity is at our hearts, pressing upon our time-torn lives, warming us with intimations of an astounding destiny, calling us home unto Itself" (29). All we need to do is listen.

In a world tyrannized by time, a host of people have been wounded. Suffering often turns inward under the pressure of incessant demands. We bury our needs, our hurts, and our pain. The trouble is, buried pain doesn't die. It congeals, gathers force, and spawns new pain. It works from the roots of a person's spirit outward, constantly colliding with the pressures of the world until the tension mounts unbearably. To this very world, this world of the furious swirl, this world for which Jesus was wounded and bruised, we bring our faith, a message, and an action of healing grace.

THE OGRE OF THE UNUSUAL

The privatization of pain in the modern world, which provides so few avenues for expressing one's need, leads to a second threat to a renewed faith: the ogre of the unusual. Often, the way a modern person learns to live with pain is to domesticate it. We can subdue it by routines and orderly living.

In "The Love Song of J. Alfred Prufrock," T. S. Eliot tells the story of an unusual little man who has been invited to a party. He is terrified of going, for he fears that his inner being will be exposed for all to see. Thus, for a time, he takes some comfort in the fact that he will "prepare a face to meet the faces that we meet." A pale and ineffective comfort, this. We don masks to meet the masks of others. We bury our grief, hide our loneliness, domesticate our despair. Thus we try to appear comfortable while discomfort eats us from the inside out.

Modern society prizes nothing quite so much as the image—the appearance of success and achievement, the sense that all is right and orderly in the world. The problem is the image is only that—an appearance. Beneath the thin veneer of order seethe decidedly disorderly lives. We are seldom if ever permitted to reveal the chaos of personal pain. It is unseemly, a bit uncouth or improper, to admit to disorder in a world in which women are expected to be Barbie and men are ordered to be Ken—unrumpled, neat, successful. Especially they are expected to be *successful,* evidenced by the proper houses, automobiles, clothing, and toys, all of which are carefully tailored by the images popularized by our culture. It helps to be good-looking and well-built also, for which ends health clubs and tanning parlors and the like proliferate as multimillion dollar enterprises. Image is everything.

What determines the image? Advertising—a world that unearths our desires and links them to products. But also an entire way of life, fueled by expectations according to what a consumer society deems as success. A consumer society, all too often, consumes lives. In this rage for propriety, what do we do with our pain? Pain and suffering do not fit the image, after all. They mark one as unusual—one who doesn't conform to the public mask. Under the mask may lie a grimace of anguish, and few dare let it sneak through until the mask collapses and the need itself consumes the individual.

Like the wicked witch of fairy tales, modern society fears the ogre of the unusual. In the fairy-tale kingdom of children's literature, the ogre appears as a threat, a disruption of a routine. It is, of course, an imaginary being, usually depicted as a lumpish creature with hideous green skin. In a sense, each of us bears an ogre inside—this lumpish green clot of the unusual that we try to hide from others so we won't appear different. In the fairy-tale world, the ogre grows ever more powerful and fearful, until one person—often not very heroic, quite often very common—steps forward to name it, grapple with it, and defeat it. The larger terror in modern life is that our ogres remain hidden so long. Unnamed and unconfronted, they seem to grow ever more huge and threatening. We have few places to go with our pain and to name our ogres.

Unfortunately, as the urgency of confronting such ogres has grown in society, the contemporary church has increasingly ignored their presence. The church today has also become afflicted by an unwillingness to confess and confront the ogres of the unusual.

Many churches insist upon nothing quite so much as the appearance of order. With their neat orders of service, their worship structured according to tradition, their polished services in their polished buildings, these churches are threatened by and deeply afraid of the unusual. The dangerous "what if" of the unexpected is a thing to fear. It might mean the exclusion of a scheduled hymn, the lengthening of a carefully planned hour of worship. In effect, these bodies have created a world in the image of their own advertised selves: "God is with us; all is well with the world."

In fact, when God is with us we discover that all is indeed not well with the world. Jesus moved at the depths of people's need. Jesus moved where pain lived, where ogres flourished. Jesus named sin, confronted it, healed it. Jesus kept few neat schedules, and was constantly interrupted by the ogres of the unusual. The only schedule he adamantly stuck to was divinely decreed before the advent of time: His ultimate confrontation with the cross upon which he vanquished ogres more terrible than we dare imagine.

If in the body of believers—those who share a communion of love with each other because of our communion of love with God—we schedule out of existence the ogres of the unusual, we have nurtured the deceit of conformity. Those afflicted by the ogres of the unusual have no place to go. They are driven to the isolation of privacy where ogres thrive. Therein also lies the third fear that inhibits spiritual renewal in the modern age: the fear of exposure of a private self in a public world.

A PRIVATE SELF IN A PUBLIC WORLD

For some odd reason, we have developed the attitude that afflicted persons are entitled to privacy. An unstated, but widely practiced law of social decorum has it that anguish is rude. One sees here a spin-off of the ogre of the unusual, whereby a person is reluctant to express need by a fear of what others may think or say or do. But this reluctance to admit private anguish into the open also seems woven into the institutional fabric of our age. Perhaps this is why the lines at the psychologists' offices are so long; they have supplanted the church's office of hearing confession. By confession, I mean exposing and opening our inner selves to others.

The source of the malady lies in our fear of breaking routine, of discomfiture. If I listen to another's need, one might think I am thereby obligated to minister to that need. And I don't have the time. Or the talent. Or the correct resources.

It is little wonder that persons are reluctant to expose their private pain. They fear a debacle of shame, a theological horror house where the world of their congregations can jeer them from the safety of their ordered lives. Consequently, the modern church has been content to let avenues of confession of private need run into a dead end. Church services are frequently rigidly ordered affairs; congregants want their one-hour spiritual infusion; like sparrows on a branch they cling to the routine of order before flying off to their "real" lives. Public exposure of private need raises the threat of disorder. Something must be done about this, after all. But what? And how? It is so much easier to keep steadfast silence.

Sometimes there is indeed good reason for silence. Certainly one must be very careful to whom one makes confession. A number of times I have witnessed persons revealing their inmost heartaches, pain, and sin to someone they thought they could trust, only to have that trust violated through the maliciousness of gossip—one of Satan's most formidable tools to subvert Christian love.

What is one to do, then? If one does not have a trusted confessor, or an experienced personal support group, it is essential that the church provide a channel for such grace, albeit far more discreetly than it sometimes has in the past. Some churches are accustomed to having people gather at the altar for prayer, but this kind of openness and embrace of God's communal love is increasingly rare. When it does occur, too often it appears as a spectacle—a scene for congregants to look upon as some sort of spiritual entertainment. It is far better, it seems to me, to provide the opportunity for confession in some place and at another time than public worship. For example, one church in our area saw the need for such confession and offered it as part of the worship service. Out of the audience of nearly two thousand, not one person came forward. But surely the hurts were there. Two thousand people with neither sin nor pain? Quickly, the church took two different steps. One was to provide prayer rooms in another area of the church where individuals could meet with a small group of elders and prayer warriors of the church. Once the door of that room closed, absolute confidentiality ruled. The second step was to offer an altogether alternative service on Saturday evening. My wife and I have attended a number of those services, also attended by street people, those in rehab centers—in fact, anyone who feels the need for God's forgiving grace. Here the very nature of the service is different. Testimonies are given. It is not unusual for the senior pastor to preach in jeans. The organ and grand piano are set aside for a Christian band. The point is that the church *reaches out* to those who need confession.

But there is one other hindrance to confession in our churches today.

Mandated to honesty, most of us would also admit that we are afraid to have others reveal their needs *to us*. We may very well have little skill or understanding of the problems set forth. We are bothered by our own spiritual inadequacy. Many years ago my wife endured a seven-week hospitalization for a biochemically induced postpartum depression. Just recently one of her acquaintances confessed *her* need to my wife. "I just thought you would want to keep your illness private," the person said.

A lack of knowledge is almost as deadly as a lack of understanding. Because we fear our own inadequacy we recoil from the needs of others. But anyone can comfort and pray. Most often that's all that is required of us. To be there.

Here, then, are three threats to one's newfound faith and the need for new foundations. Oppressed by the tyranny of time, the modern Christian finds a schedule clogged to bursting. We find it hard enough to discover time for personal relaxation and needs, let alone ministering to the needs of others. The necessary response here is to discover and use our individual gifts. This gives us the spiritual freedom to say no to certain things, but ultimately it is a powerful yes to a new spiritual freedom.

Afflicted by the ogre of the unusual, the modern Christian, furthermore, often dares not admit to personal need. In the glitter and gloss of our world of images, we find a certain safety in conformity. Thereby we bury our ogres ever more deeply in our souls, where they gather strength and threaten to destroy us. It is absolutely essential to the renewed foundation of our faith that we establish a community of trust, accepting of change and of the unusual. While this is a corporate aim of the body of Christ, it must begin individually, in each of our hearts.

Finally, as a church we have a fear of the public exposure of personal pain. Whether it is considered a breach of decorum, a fracture in the mask that all is well in the world, or a threat to our personal involvement, confession or admission of personal need has found little place in the highly organized liturgies of our public worship. We have to discover new ways of meeting those needs in order to build the foundations of corporate worship. That forms a basic step toward joy that we discover from the Israelites—rebuilding the temple itself.

CHAPTER 5

Building Spiritual Foundations

Reading: Ezra 3:7—4:5

The first step toward rebuilding a broken spiritual life is the act of renewal before God. The action does not necessarily involve a physical altar. It may be as simple as going to your knees at a bedside or finding any quiet place by yourself. Perhaps it occurs in your personal devotions, where you let God's words come to you. Be still. Listen. Perhaps walking in sandaled feet across dew-splashed grass. Beads like diamonds cling to the blades. A light breeze touches the roses in the garden and suddenly they are crowns of color full of love, hope, faith. The altar may be any place you are alone with God. You feel the breath of heaven in your face.

This meeting with God in our lives is not always, however, in such moments of calm repose. Too often our pleas stick in our throats when we call out to God. The noise and confusion that attack us render our words meaningless. We no longer know what to say or what to pray for. We are not alone in that. David confesses in Psalm 6:6 that, "I am worn out from groaning." What he meant by that is clear—the harsh, needled pain of longing for an answer.

Coming to the altar is the act of seeking your Savior, of opening your life to him, and of asking him to come. He will come. Perhaps not in a cataclysm of thunder and lightning, perhaps not with signs and wonders. Jesus said that a "wicked and adulterous generation asks for a miraculous sign" (Matt. 12:39). What he asks of us is the altar of an open heart. There he can utter the most tender of whispers: "You are my child. I love you dearly."

The existential religions pervasive today may sound appealing because of their promises of personal fulfillment, personal success, and personal peace of mind, but they are alien to Christianity. Christianity is a love-driven religion that flows outward to others rather than inward to the self. In Christianity personal fulfillment is loving God with all one's heart and soul and mind and strength; personal success is loving your neighbor as yourself; peace of mind is living in faithfulness to the law of God. Love cannot be isolated; it cannot be something gathered and clutched to one's breast. Love is corporate. In Christianity it occurs first in the body of believers, as our sacrifice at the altar is nurtured in the family of God.

If the first step toward spiritual wholeness is a recovery of devotional intimacy as individuals before God, that in itself does not solve the dilemma of the exiled spirit of the Israelites, nor does it solve ours. Our faith is not solitary. It is not only a relationship between us and God, although that certainly is the essential starting point. Christianity, like the people of Israel, is a community of love and brotherhood. If God's Spirit reaches into the believer's heart, it is so that the believer may reach out to the hearts of others.

Maybe that sounds like a platitude—a thin wisp of pretty thoughts as insubstantial as a haze that flickers through our minds. After all, as we discussed in the last chapter, we are all busy people. Nonetheless, this reaching out to others is grounded in real actions.

I have known Nicole Thrasher a good portion of her life since she grew up just around the corner from us and went to school with my son. Since her earliest years Nicole felt the call of the Lord on her life to missions. After graduating from a high school for the academically gifted, and then from a university, it would seem the whole world was open to Nicole. Indeed it was. The Lord led her to direct an orphanage in the shattered eastern European country of Albania. Not until the collapse of the Soviet Union did the West become aware of the dictatorial persecution of that country and its people. When the curtain finally did open on that horror show, it disclosed hundreds of displaced, starving children. It was to them that God led Nicole.

The chaos in Albania was far from over with the fall of the Soviet Union. Following the economic collapse in 1996, armed raiders took to the streets, burning, looting, and engaging in gun battles. When violence erupted, Americans were evacuated from the country. As the fighting encroached upon the orphanage, officials urged Nicole and her fellow American workers to leave. But this was the place God had sent them. They stayed. I have a copy of a newsletter Nicole's mother prepared for those supporting her in prayer. In it appears a picture of one of the orphans, holding his hands full of spent shells from the gun battles that occurred right in front of the orphanage. Yet while the city burned, the orphanage was protected.

This place, this small orphanage in a "ravaged land," was truly Nicole's church. The church is never simply a building. It is the body of believers living together as Christ directs them.

OUTWARD FROM THE ALTAR

Appropriately, Sheshbazzar and Zerubbabel set about building the altar first. That act proclaimed to the tribes around them: "Here we take our stand. We are the Lord's people." The next task was to make this action permanent by housing the sacred altar in a temple of worship. Thus they turned their attention to rebuilding the ruined foundations of the temple. It was a daunting, physical task. The Babylonians had destroyed everything to heaps of jagged rock. Space had to be cleared. Land dug free. New stones hewn and hauled. Logs of cedar were ferried by sea from Lebanon to Joppa and then carted overland. Provisions had to be made for the laborers. And, of course, there were always those marauding tribes to be concerned about. For five hard years the Israelites labored at their task. As happened in so many of these affairs, curious twists of history occurred as God worked out his plan.

For example, immediately after the altar was rebuilt and the pattern of sacrifices reestablished, the men set to work on the foundations for the temple. In short order they had the space cleared and the foundations laid. It was only the sign of a promise, merely the first primitive step. But it was a sign; it was a step, and the people rejoiced: "Here will be the house of the Lord! It is not only a dream; it's becoming a reality." So with the foundations laid, they paused for a moment of celebration and festivity. Some of the people shouted in jubilation. Some of the elderly wept loudly. Why would they weep? Some commentators say it is because they remembered the glory of Solomon's temple, and that this one would never match its splendor. Possibly. I think they wept with the pure emotional joy of having found their true home once again. They had for many years been strangers in a strange land. Now they were truly home in the Lord's house.

Almost at the very moment of jubilation, however, the scene started to shift as the enemies of the Israelites came sneaking out of the wilderness. Their first ploy was to tell Zerubbabel that they wanted to help out with the work and sacrifices. Zerubbabel and Jeshua curtly turned them down: "You have no part with us in building a temple to our God. We alone will build it for the LORD, the God of Israel" (Ezra 4:3). The offer may have been tempting to the Israelites, short-handed and overworked as they were. Surely, however, Zerubbabel sensed two things. First, the "outsiders" had their own plan to insinuate their way into the spiritual heart of the Israelites. Second, the Israelites were God's called people, and as such no task was too large or too daunting.

Zerubbabel's response also has profound implications for our own altars. Any of us could quickly list a half-dozen threats to renewed spiritual commitment. Some may be internal struggles against lifelong patterns of sin—lust, envy, pride, and the like. Some may be external threats—disrespect of friends or coworkers, or a lack of resources to develop one's faith, for example. In the latter area, one thinks particularly of Christians in the former Soviet Union, where resources to nurture their faith simply were not there. The Russian poet Irina Ratushinskaya, for example, a survivor of the Soviet prison camps, was converted as a child but did not have a copy of the Bible until she was in her early twenties.

We shiver when we think of the opportunities we have to nurture our communal faith. We cringe when we think of how often we neglect those opportunities. It helps to reflect for a moment on what the word *community* actually means. It has always been a part of our Christian vocabulary.

Our modern word for community derives from the Latin *communicare,* meaning "to hold in common." Thus the commu-nity of the church begins with a set of beliefs we hold in common. Although some elements may differ according to tra-dition and practice, the fundamentals are the same: We are sinners in need of grace. Jesus is the incarnate Son of God. He

died on the cross to forgive our sins. He was resurrected from the
dead so that we, the children of God, might also be resurrected
to eternal life.

These fundamental beliefs place us in communion with
fellow believers. Basic sacraments further bind us in communion with God. Through baptism we enter a sacred
covenant. We, or we in the name of our children, seal a set
of promises—giving ours to God, receiving his to us.
Through the Lord's Supper we enter communion with God,
affirming that he died for our sins and saved us from them.
To share our fundamental beliefs and partake of the sacraments, we have reason enough to enter the community of
believers in worship.

In *The Purpose Driven Life*, Rick Warren emphasizes the cen-
trality of regular worship and membership in a church body for
our individual lives:

> Membership in the family of God is neither
> inconsequential nor something to be casually
> ignored. The church is God's agenda for the
> world. Jesus said, *"I will build my church, and all
> the powers of hell will not conquer it."* The church is
> indestructible and will exist for eternity. It will
> outlive this universe, and so will your role in it.
> The person who says, "I don't need the church,"
> is either arrogant or ignorant....
>
> The Bible calls the church *"the bride of Christ"*
> and *"the body of Christ."* I can't imagine saying to
> Jesus, "I love you, but I dislike your wife." Or "I
> accept you, but I reject your body." But we do
> this whenever we dismiss or demean or complain
> about the church.... The Bible says, *"Love your
> spiritual family."* Sadly, many Christians *use* the
> church but don't love it. (132)

How do we understand this church fellowship, which, sometimes, we don't seem to love at all? Warren continues by suggesting several reasons.

First, writes Warren, "A church family identifies you as a genuine believer" (133). The church my wife and I attend is only a block east of our home. As we walk together to services on a Sunday morning, I can't help being aware of our neighbors—mowing their lawns, washing cars, packing the van for a day at the beach. I genuinely like my neighbors. We're friendly. We watch each other's houses and take in the mail during vacations. Sometimes, in time of need, we mow each other's lawns or bring in meals. But on Sunday mornings, this is what we are: believers going to worship. I hope that is evident on other days as well.

Second, Warren argues that church fellowship "moves you out of self-centered isolation" (133). Basically, we shift attention from ourselves to others. Earlier we discussed the discovery of gifts and ministries as a means to direct our time. If you attend a worship service in a genuine, Bible-believing church some Sunday morning, you'll discover that there is no shortage of needs to direct your energy away from yourself. But we don't need experiences alone to tell us. Such parables as "The Sheep and the Goats" (Matt. 25:11–40) and "The Good Samaritan" (Luke 10:30–36) make Jesus' wishes unmistakably clear.

It was the custom when my grandfather was a minister that he and the elders would adjourn to the council room following the morning service. There they would light up pipes and cheap cigars and discuss the finer theological points of the sermon. Grandfather, of course, was always given the final word. Times have changed culturally, but the idea remains sound. In worship we gather to hear God's will for our lives. We discuss that further in personal small groups. We exercise our spiritual muscle by the readings we do, the music we listen to, the devotions we engage in.

Warren lists several other reasons to be a part of a church community. For example, he points out that the church provides a means for sharing in "Christ's mission in the world" (135). Thereby we participate in Jesus' Great Commission to go into all the world and make disciples (see Matt. 28:19–20). Furthermore, the church functions as a means of discipline. The church stands for what is right in God's sight. Therefore, it bears responsibility to correct people whose vision turns inward upon themselves as their first priority.

It is both all too easy and also all too wrong to lament the ills of the modern church. The errors and sins that afflict Christians individually and communally sometimes glare like aberrant torches in modern culture. In turn, modern culture tends to subject the church to mockery and condemnation. In many modern circles, Christians are by definition deluded fools. The persecution of the church, while seldom to the degree of the early martyrs, still exists in a vast cultural snobbishness that decries religion as a psychological crutch. We Christians, in many cultural circles, are the lamed people, hobbling along through life barely half alive.

While the church is an easy target, and no less free from fallen nature than any other organization, this peculiar cultural malignancy is hard to understand. Our culture celebrates tolerance in all things—except Christianity. Why is this? Simply because the church is a source for God's absolutes. It is the repository of truth and ethical verities. In an age of relativism, that is not a popular place to be.

But the Christian church is not now, nor has it ever been, about popularity. It is all about bringing people into a deep personal relationship with Truth itself. The fundamentals of our faith—that we are sinners and need a savior, that Jesus enacted our salvation on the cross, that by turning to him we have eternal life—do not change. In its task of testifying to and protecting those fundamentals, the Christian church engages an utterly heroic task. I have worshipped in dozens of churches—some tiny clapboard affairs, some opulent cathedrals—but the heart of the church, the glue of our community, is the proclamation that our God reigns. No matter the setting, my soul still thrills to hear that message. As long as that message is preached and heard and heeded, the church shall not fail. Despite persecution, mockery, and the boiling forces of relativism, our God reigns, and his church, his bride, will stand before him triumphant.

In C. S. Lewis's *The Screwtape Letters,* the devil Screwtape reveals an uncanny knowledge of the nature of God as he instructs his nephew Wormwood. Essentially, the book is a penetrating insight into the reality of the Christian life and the ways that superficial or false teachings seduce us. But in this matter of worship, Screwtape makes a comment that we would do well to inscribe upon our mental altars: "When He talks about losing their selves, He means only abandoning the clamour of self-will; once they have done that, He really gives them back all their personality, and boasts (I am afraid, sincerely) that when they are wholly His they will be more themselves than ever" (65).

It would be a tragic mistake to ignore a final reason for communal worship, for in our world of cataclysmic events and harrowing change we need to gather together to receive courage from the Lord. For some reason, courage is seldom mentioned in today's worship, even when the need for it has in no way diminished through the centuries. Surely our lives are more *comfortable* than ever before, but they are also more *complicated*—and therefore more fragile.

Courage from the Lord is one of the great themes of the Bible. If the Bible is to have any relevance to our lives today, we have to grasp that theme. I am not saying we are spiritual cowards; I am saying we get lulled into a false sense of security based on the things we have rather than on God's authority. If not cowards, we often are—when we pause to think about it—scared stiff. What if those things disappeared this morning? What if I go to work and my office is cleared out? What if my medical appointment this afternoon reveals I have six months to live? What if I come home this evening and my spouse has left? Life is fragile. We need a sense of security that at once undergirds and transcends temporal events.

In his parting words to Joshua and the Israelites, Moses stressed God's backing as they were about to enter a strange land: "Be strong and courageous. Do not be afraid or terrified because of them, for the LORD your God goes with you; he will never leave you nor forsake you" (Deut. 31:6–7). After Moses died, the mantle of leadership fell upon Joshua. What a terrifying task. But three times in the early verses of Joshua 1, God affirmed to him to be courageous because "I will never leave you nor forsake you" (v. 5). There is a terrible beauty in the simplicity of that promise. It bears no addenda, no complicated conditions or clauses; it simply gives the statement of fact.

Move ahead in history to the time frame we are considering in this study. Hezekiah, one of the last kings of Judah, was also one of the best and most noble kings. Yes, he did succumb to pride in his later years, and, yes, that did separate him from communion with God (see 2 Chron. 32:24–26). But he was faithful in restoring communal worship of God in the kingdom, aided greatly by the prophet Isaiah. Second Chronicles states that he did "what was good and right and faithful before the LORD his God" (31:20).

Right at that moment, when everything seemed secure, the Assyrian king Sennacherib came and invaded Judah (701 BC). Despite the ominous force, Hezekiah prepared his men for battle and encouraged them with these words:

> Be strong and courageous. Do not be afraid or discouraged because of the king of Assyria and the vast army with him, for there is a greater power with us than with him. With him is only the arm of flesh, but with us is the LORD our God to help us and to fight our battles. (32:7–8)

There lies communal courage, because they were a community united under God.

Here's the rest of the story. Sennacherib stood outside the gates, mocking God's people. Worse, he derided the Lord God himself, lowering him to the level of common idols. Hezekiah and Isaiah knew where to turn. They knelt and prayed: "And the LORD sent an angel, who annihilated all the fighting men and the leaders and officers in the camp of the Assyrian king" (32:21). That is the God who is the source of our courage.

Skip now to Ezra, having heard of the rebuilding of the ruins of Jerusalem. Constantly, threats and frustrations assailed Zerubbabel and the leaders.

Several years ago I took my son to a batting cage, where you bat against a machine inside a net. For some odd reason my machine started sending the balls at shorter and shorter intervals. It seemed to me like two were coming at me at once. Sure enough, when I was done a sign went up: Out of Order. Ezra's life was out of order. But then King Artaxerxes intervened, providing the finances for work to continue. "Praise be to the LORD," said Ezra, "who has put it into the king's heart to bring honor to the house of the LORD.... I took courage and gathered leading men from Israel to go up with me" (Ezra 7:27–28).

The call to courage has not been left in the dust of ancient history. It too formed a central theme of the New Testament church. Jesus spoke the peace of courage into the hearts of his disciples. Walking on the lake under dark skies, he approached his "terrified" disciples in their boat and said, "Take courage! It is I. Don't be afraid" (Matt. 14:27). When Paul was imprisoned, the Lord appeared to him and said, "'Take courage! As you have testified about me in Jerusalem, so you must also testify in Rome'" (Acts 23:11). The Lord had a plan for Paul; he also gave him the courage to do it.

Under increasing persecution, the early leaders of the church took up the theme. When Paul was shipwrecked in a storm off Malta, he said to the crew of the ship, "Keep up your courage, men, for I have faith in God that it will happen just as he told me" (Acts 27:25). And there's the heart of this entire theme, in every instance we have noted. We can take courage because of our faith in God.

Other passages appear where the word of courage is spoken to build up the community of the early church. In 1 Corinthians 16:13 Paul wrote to the church, "Stand firm in the faith; be men of courage." The writer of Hebrews tells us that we are God's house, "if we hold on to our courage and the hope of which we boast" (3:6). What is that hope in which we boast? Above all it consists of those fundamental tenets of our faith that we outlined earlier. But in this matter of taking courage, no testimony stands more clear than that of Paul in Romans 8:38–39: "For I am convinced that neither death nor life, neither angels nor demons, neither the present nor the future, nor any powers, neither height nor depth, nor anything else in all creation, will be able to separate us from the love of God that is in Christ Jesus our Lord." Therein lies our ultimate hope and courage. We are the body of Christ, to be resurrected and to live eternally with him.

As we meet for worship we recognize that our spiritual community holds many things in common. Sacraments bind us together. Patterns of worship identify us as believers and instill knowledge of God. As we take our faith outward *into* the world, however, we need courage to hold fast to our faith. We want to authenticate our faith. As Ezra directed the spiritual development in Jerusalem, he too confronted the same challenge.

CHAPTER 6

People of Authentic Faith

Reading: Ezra 6—7

Every Christian longs for an "authentic" faith. We all want the "real thing" if we're serious about this business of being a Christian. We've had it with pretending and acting; we've had enough of the superficial. But how do we gauge an authentic faith? How do we know our relationship with the living God is indeed alive? So often we bang our spiritual heads against a thick, dark wall of questions: "How do I get there? What do I have to do? What are the secrets?" We begin to believe that on the other side of a door lie answers, but someone else holds the keys. We just keep knocking until our knuckles wear out. By searching passages of Persian and Israelite history, some answers come to light.

THE LONGING

No one could accuse Darius of being weak-minded once he decided to take a position on an issue. Tattenai, a governor of Trans-Euphrates (all the Persian holdings west of the Euphrates River) had sent a letter to Darius, asking the king to decide a dispute between the Israelites and their neighbors. After a search of the royal archives that located Cyrus's original decree, Darius not only reaffirmed Cyrus's original decree but also added to it three stipulations. First, no one, including the governor, is to interfere in the work. Second, taxes and tribute from Trans-Euphrates will support the work. Third, if anyone violates stipulations one and two, they are to die.

This was a pretty significant incentive—so much so that the rebuilding of the temple was completed in 516 BC, exactly seventy years following its destruction.

Truly the people celebrated then. They sacrificed, praised God, and danced well into the night. But something more had to come to fill the temple; besides the joy of praise it had to contain the weight of God's presence. Then as now, God's revelation of himself occurs through his Word. Then as now, celebrants in the temple needed to fix their faith in the eternal foundation of God's revelation for right living with him. The law of God must be taught. It came then in the form of a teacher living in Babylon. The Israelites needed Ezra to authenticate their faith.

Ezra arrived in Jerusalem in 458 BC. An interesting and not insignificant detail emerges in the chronology of Israel here. The temple was completed in 516 BC. Ezra did not arrive in Jerusalem with his supporting band of exiles until 458 BC. What was going on during this seventy-seven-year period? We have precious few details of what was happening in Jerusalem, but in the Persian Empire God was preparing a course of events that would lead directly to the liberation of the Jews held there. As so often happens, God shapes events behind what only *seems* to be reality to us. In his omniscience and eternalness he alone sees the full picture.

In this instance, we have to look at Xerxes I (Ahasuerus)

and his ascension to the Persian throne in the year 486 BC. His father, Darius I, had just undergone the costly Greek wars, leading to his defeat at Marathon. It was this same Ahasuerus who took Esther as his bride in 479 BC. We are probably all familiar with the story of Esther, surely one of the most dramatic in all the Bible, as she risked her life to expose Haman and save the Jews whom he wanted to slaughter. Haman desired nothing less than a complete genocide, and there was only this one faithful, strong-hearted woman to stand in the gap. If we remember the story, we also know the ending— how Haman was hanged on the gallows he intended for Esther's cousin and adoptive father, Mordecai, and how the Jewish feast of Purim was instituted as a celebration in 473 BC. The well-being and theological tradition of the Jews was thereby preserved.

Behind the scenes, then, God prepared a solid continuity in the Israelites' faith. He allowed them freedom from distress and freedom to establish and maintain their traditional laws and rituals. More important, clearly, was that knowledge of God's law for righteous living.

When Ezra arrived at Jerusalem he brought with him three unique contributions. First, and most important, he was an outstanding scholar-teacher of God's laws (see Ezra 7:6). It was essential now for the Israelites to have the solid legal foundation of God's laws on which to build their faith. They were a people notorious for slipping and sliding off that foundation. Second, Ezra also brought a support system of Levitical priests, temple servants, choirs, and the like. No one person can unify a people as diverse in personalities or callings as the Israelites. Ezra's support system was essential to put authentic faith into effect. The third important contribution was, oddly enough, a commission from the great King Artaxerxes, successor to Xerxes I.

THE COMMISSION

As was the custom of the day, a band of travelers as large as Ezra's would bear some official document from a high-ranking government official authorizing the trip. In this case, the document was from the king himself. Historically, that authorization bears several interesting implications. First of all, Artaxerxes freely permits the Israelites to go. No contingencies, no stipulations. They are to be given complete religious freedom (see Ezra 7:13). Second, the king himself supports their religion with a freewill offering to buy all the necessary resources for future work (see vv. 15–17). Moreover, Artaxerxes commands other Trans-Euphrates rulers that they "have no authority to impose taxes, tribute or duty on any of the priests, Levites, singers, gatekeepers, temple servants or other workers at this house of God" (v. 24).

This last point may be particularly interesting to us today, for it is the first time in Scripture where a foreign state holding authority over the Israelites establishes the policy of no taxes on a religious institution. It was as essential for Artaxerxes to see that stipulation in order for the Israelite church to flourish as it is for modern political leaders to see it for the church to flourish. It represents the first biblical reference to the separation of church and state, a concept affirmed by Jesus (see Matt. 22:15–22).

If we probe deeper into this document, more interesting items emerge. One of the important ones for the church is freedom from persecution. Not only does Artaxerxes assure this personally, but he also commands it for the governors of Trans-Euphrates. We modern believers tend to think of persecution of the church as a phenomenon of communist and third-world countries—and indeed it is. The horror stories seep into the West, but they seem strangely muted to us by simple distance. Yet one may well contend that our own nation, despite its constitutional protection, has hardly been free from religious persecution.

So urgent is this point for contemporary Christians that it deserves a moment's further reflection.

Here's one example from the not too distant past. My father's early years were spent as the son of a minister in areas of Iowa. Some of those areas were heavily populated by German and Dutch immigrants. My grandfather, who was born in Germany, had the good fortune to be proficient in three languages—German, Dutch, and English. For a number of years he had to preach separate services in all three. My father had to sit through each of them!

When World War I broke out, so did a wave of anti-German sentiment across the United States. My father recalls being mercilessly taunted by former school friends. When a parade was held in the town of Grundy Center, Iowa, where they were then living, one of the oldest German men in the town was forced to walk at the head of the parade waving the American flag. He dared not stumble or fall. Then Governor Harding of Iowa issued his own decree. All those German pastors (of whom there were many in Iowa, especially toward the so-called "German Valley" area along the Mississippi River) had to translate their sermons into English. For my grandfather this wasn't difficult. But for many older pastors who had never mastered English it was a terrible burden. Some sat for hours trying to translate their native tongue into a language they barely understood.

While such cases are overt and, it may be argued, the result of the perversity of human nature rather than systematic persecution, a far more subtle and dangerous form of persecution has crept into American society today. I am not thinking here of the media, although surely a good argument could be made in that case. Rather, I am thinking in particular of the systematic rejection of religious thinking and Christianity in universities and in the courts of this land. While higher education has raced to embrace every new cause, it has relegated Christianity to no more than a historical footnote. In fact, in some institutions it is considered a sign of weakness of mind to bring one's faith to bear upon one's study. In others, it is a tenable cause for losing your job. Similarly, systematic attacks upon religious traditions occur almost yearly in the courts.

It is not simply a matter of opposition to belief, although it is all of that. A former student of mine, now studying in graduate school, commented to me that there is tolerance of every belief *except* Christianity. Why is this so? For one thing, Christianity is about belief, a lifestyle, and a mission. Prestigious universities offer courses that openly subvert Christianity. As I write this, the University of Michigan is preparing to offer a humanities course titled "How to be Gay." Self-interest governs many curricula, whereas, as Charles Colson and Nancy Pearcy write in *How Now Shall We Live?* "Our major task in life is to discover what is true and to live in step with that truth" (14). They add that "we are either contributing to the broken condition of the world or participating with God in transforming the world to reflect his righteousness. We are either advancing the rule of Satan or establishing the reign of God" (13). No wonder we confront systematic opposition: Christianity is the most dangerous force at work in the world today. It seeks nothing less than to transform the world. It can't be stated any more clearly than Jesus did: "For God so loved the world that he gave his one and only Son, that whoever believes in him shall not perish but have eternal life" (John 3:16). Love, in all the fullness of its meaning and implications, has become a word scarcely recognized by the world.

What is the contemporary Christian to do?

Maybe Ezra and Nehemiah didn't have the secular gate-keepers of today blocking the Word of God, but they did have those annoying foreigners buzzing around the gates and ridiculing their belief. Maybe the Israelites didn't have secularists telling them to keep their temple a long way from the courthouse, but they did soon have people defiling the new altar, treating it their way instead of God's way. And maybe Ezra and Nehemiah didn't have windy sophists telling them to keep their nasty values off the world of "objective," scientific data, but they did have worldly temptations beating away at the gates of the city. Even while the Israelites chanted their temple praise, some of them were listening to a siren song in the back of their heads with lyrics of money, sex, and power.

The problem with those now enrolled in the High Church of Postmodernism is that (1) they have so many gatekeepers that they have to keep out anything smacking of values, or (2) they avow a tolerance that lets anything that means less than something in. What an excruciating pew to sit in. One wears the heavy woolen suit woven out of every fashionable thread, yet one has to keep squirming left and right to see that no mention of ethics or inviolable truth comes slinking down the aisle like some invasive and infectious bacterium. Let one word of God in, and it might change us all.

They're right. It just might. It's all so very uncomfortable.

A final implication appears in this passage. Having received the king's edict, Ezra is quick to praise the Authority behind the king: "Praise be to the LORD, the God of our fathers, who has put it into the king's heart to bring honor to the house of the LORD in Jerusalem in this way" (7:27). The passage encourages us to remember that there is a higher authority over any earthly power, and that God can change the heart of any person. During the present state of affairs in higher education, we do well to pray for and support the

Christian colleges in this nation. They struggle to keep the light of God's truth alive in a world where higher education is often a confused and bedimmed mess.

Our first gauge of authentic faith, then, is *to see beyond present circumstances and acknowledge that God is the highest authority.* If we recognize that he works in our lives to work his perfect plan for us, we also believe that he does indeed have the complete power and authority to execute that plan.

THE REVELATION

Ezra's band of exiles camped by the Ahava Canal, which flowed into the Euphrates River, in preparation for their long and dangerous trek across the desert. A nine-hundred-mile journey lay before them, through treacherous land where roving bandits preyed upon caravans like theirs. Like raving hyenas, they could smell out a group of defenseless travelers. Perhaps the most fearful part of such a journey is the very act of setting out, knowing what might lie in store.

Ezra had possibilities for protection. Artaxerxes had offered his aid; soldiers and horsemen were available for protection. I admit that I would have asked for them. If I were a foot soldier in today's army, heading into enemy territory, I would like to have a column of tanks and armored personnel carriers. It would be good to have squadrons of attack helicopters scouting out the land too. This was not Ezra's way. He called the people to fast in order to draw closer to God. Ezra himself confessed that he was ashamed to ask the king for horsemen and soldiers, "because we had told the king, 'The gracious hand of our God is on everyone who looks to him, but his great anger is against all who forsake him'" (8:22). So they fasted and prayed. God answered. It took Ezra four months to make the journey. As Ezra noted:

"The hand of our God was on us, and he protected us from enemies and bandits along the way" (v. 31). Here, then, we see the second gauge of authentic faith. If the first is to see beyond immediate circumstances and to acknowledge the sole authority of God, the second is *to rely upon that authority alone for our actions, exclusive of any other power.*

When he arrived in Jerusalem, however, Ezra faced a new challenge—not physical, but spiritual. The enemy now was not a party of desert bandits; it was the human heart held in bondage to sin. In this particular case it was the sin of intermarriage with pagan neighbors, a violation of God's express warnings. Too often that path had been taken; too often it had led to worship of pagan gods. This is what had happened in the sacred city during those seventy-seven years. Once again the people had to be called to repentance.

The third stage to authentic faith is *to hold on to God's law as his perfect directions for faithful living.* That is our response to his plan and his power. By that we affirm our living relationship with a loving God, who gave these laws, as he himself declared, because he loves us.

However much we cherish the ideals of justice, order, and truth in both our personal and social lives, the fact is that we often react negatively to individual laws themselves. The best testimony to fallen nature is the nature of humanity itself.

One such instance, for example, might be when you see the lights flashing in the rearview mirror. Adrenaline surges the length of your body. You glance down and see that you're doing fourteen over the speed limit. Not a chance for a break on this one. When you cool down, you realize it's not so much the law you hate but the fact that you got caught breaking it and had to pay the penalty. A forgotten truth hits you: We could not live sanely (or long) in a society without a pattern of laws.

God gives his divine law to maintain a loving and lasting relationship with us. We can gauge the authenticity of our own faith by how we walk in that law and thereby maintain a relationship with God. But honesty compels us to admit that steps of faith are sometimes like boulders to clamber over. Our human condition too often leaves us feeling that God's law is only words and the loving relationship is a distorted memory.

Three lessons for authentic faith appear, then, as Ezra arrives at Jerusalem. The first test of our own faith is whether we see beyond the bewildering maze of our present circumstances and acknowledge that God is the highest authority. This test asserts our confidence and our trust in God alone. The second test is whether we rely upon God's authority for all our decisions and actions. The problem here is that we want to impose our solution on a problem. After all, we know what's best for us. In fact, what's best for us is looking beyond our solutions and powers to what God would have us do. The third test, then, is whether we look to God's law, clearly outlined in the Bible, as the perfect directions for our lives. When we subordinate personal desires to God's will, we indeed live in authentic faith.

THE RESPONSE FROM THE OTHER SIDE

We all experience those times when we feel individually distanced from God, particularly during times when we undergo the trials of emotional loss or mental stress. We might feel abandoned by the God working in our history, wonder why the God of authority seems to do so little in our present lives, and find God's law little more than dusty words. Many of us experience times when we begin to believe, like Job, that God has simply disappeared from our personal landscape.

At such times—times none of us can escape—how on earth does divine law bring order and comfort? "Comfort, comfort my people, says your God," wrote Isaiah (40:1). Sometimes comfort seems like a hiss of escaping air, and we're left alone and breathless in a world of despair. One of the formative authors of my faith has been St. John of the Cross, particularly his book *Dark Night of the Soul.* What moves me powerfully in this brief work is how St. John grappled with the gritty reality of life in order to find God's comfort. Living in sixteenth-century Spain, St. John had good reason to search for comfort. Because of his religious beliefs, he was kidnapped, dragged off to the priory at Toledo, Spain, and locked up in a foul, flea-infested closet. Every so often he was pulled out and beaten mercilessly, leaving his body broken and crippled for life. After eight months of such treatment, he escaped from the tower window by tying bedsheets together. When St. John writes about suffering, I believe him.

What St. John found in his case was that suffering turned him from concern with things of this world to what he calls "contemplation." Unlike the yoga-induced, navel-gazing mysticism so popular today, this contemplation always turns outward: "For contemplation is naught else than a secret, peaceful and loving infusion from God, which, if it be permitted, enkindles in the soul the spirit of love" (72). We want to kick against suffering and drive it away. But in our fallen state we can't; we look for that "loving infusion" from God like a pillar of fire to lead us through it.

This was no less the case with the Israelites. Ezra's revelation comprised more than a set of rules; it revealed three important truths that ground our faith, even in the heart of suffering. Ezra's truths may be extended to practical applications. They may be seen as God's response to our efforts to live out an authentic faith.

AUTHORITY

The Israelites had no firm sense of authority since the time of their own kings. As we search through the "good" kings, we see that every one is qualified in some way as "doing what is right in the eyes of the Lord." Every bad king does "what is right in his own eyes." The implication is clear. Those good kings recognized the authority of God over the kingdom, they listened to the prophets, they supported the temple and the altar. Every bad king was saturated with a pride that took no notice of God. They slaughtered prophets and priests to shut up their annoying noise. They let strange altars and idols festoon the holy rooms of the temple. The worst of them worshipped at the feet of those altars.

As a consequence, spiritual stability in the kingdom grew as shaky as the political instability. And when the Babylonians led this browbeaten people into exile, there was nothing more for them than slavery under a foreign king.

Two amazing things happen when Ezra revealed the authority of God—repentance and forgiveness. Here in the law the people found very specifically what they had done wrong. Without the law they had little sense of right or wrong. It was merely a matter of whatever the king said was right at the time. Now Ezra detailed the ethical, moral standards of the king whose authority is absolute. However, when Ezra brought the law, he also brought the means for grace and forgiveness that granted restoration. He brought order.

ORDER

Our God is nothing if not an orderly God. Why? First, he is goodness—the absolute good. As the holy and good God, our Lord cannot countenance the presence of evil. Evil assaults his divine standard. Yet we also recognize that God does permit deviation from the norms he has established in order to further his kingdom work. For example, God permitted a whale to swallow Jonah to get his attention. Frogs didn't normally crawl out of the Red Sea to inundate Pharaoh's land in a wriggling and croaking green blanket. The Red Sea didn't normally part; nor the Jordan River. In such cases, we see God's intervention, not a lack of order. God is sovereign and all-powerful, but he is good in a way we can never fully comprehend.

On the other hand, the deviance, the perversion of the good and orderly things that God created is the work of Satan. Satan is a non-creator. Crafty, sly, and knowledgeable beyond our understanding, Satan can only twist and subvert what already is. Where we see order, we see God. Satan's work is to violate and distort the order God has created.

Nearly every time the prophets spoke directly in the name of God, they prefaced the words with a phrase like, "This is what the Sovereign LORD says" (Ezek. 25:15). The slim book of Jude, merely a wisp of a book, is often overlooked in the New Testament. Unfortunately so, for Jude neatly draws a parallel between the Old Testament church and the New Testament church: "For certain men whose condemnation was written about long ago have secretly slipped in among you. They are godless men, who change the grace of our God into a license for immorality and deny Jesus Christ our only Sovereign and Lord" (v. 4). Two things in particular snare my attention there. First, Jesus is identified in precise terms as sovereign and Lord. Second, as in the Ezra and Nehemiah passages, God's people are interpreting God's grace as a license to do whatever they want—that is, to engage in sin. Jude echoes Paul who wrote: "What shall we say, then? Shall we go on sinning so that grace may increase? By no means!" (Rom. 6:1–2).

The emphatic tone of both Jude and Paul arises from the fact that grace and order necessarily go hand in hand. Both of them speak against deviance—the notion that because one has grace one can live a disorderly life, following the whimsy of every deviant impulse no matter where it leads. When human whimsy takes a person, inevitably that person tramples with iron boot heels all over the good.

Ezra's great challenge, then, was to establish an orderly means for the Israelites to understand the law of the Sovereign Lord. Put simply—one needs order to understand Order. Or to put it in contemporary terms, our modern lives are governed by the order of calendars, date books, and Palm Pilots—all of which are ways of ordering our hours and protecting us against the overload of disorder. Many of us barely discern the difference. Protection against discord and chaos does not necessarily constitute order. Order is an inward state of the soul.

In his long and worthwhile book *Walden*, Henry David Thoreau packed his whole thesis into three words: "Simplicity. Simplicity. Simplicity" (102). Life, however, isn't always simple. Like untangling a twisted ball of yarn, sometimes we only make the knots tighter. But Ezra gives a surefire spiritual solution—get down to the basics with the law of God. All our traditions, all our spiritual practices, begin with that—knowledge of God's will for our lives. In fact, while the law of God provides a source of authority, and while it establishes order, above all it provides a relationship.

RELATIONSHIP

Many of us perceive human laws as rules, followed by a set of punishments for their violation. The purpose for this is social order. To a certain extent human laws do mirror God's laws, for God too provides blessing and curses accompanying his laws. Seen only as such, however, we miss entirely the spirit and biblical foundation of God's law. The very heart of God's law is to position us in a loving relationship with God who loves us.

Several things typify the relational aspect of God's revelation of his law, and it stands with the very first words of the Ten Commandments: "I am the LORD your God" (Ex. 20:2). Emphasize *your,* for God comes to the people he has selected from before time and reveals himself as their God. He initiates the covenant of love, telling them how to live in harmony with him and other humans.

We have all felt it, no doubt. That whisper of guilt when we've toed the line toward wrongdoing or that shrill noise from our conscience when we've stepped over the line. Sometimes the very foundation of our lives caves in and we can't stop the sinking. We haven't merely broken a law; we have violated a trust, twisted a dark barb into the side of a loving relationship. God's law is there to protect and preserve the relationship.

Suppose we do step over the line. Is that the end of the relationship? Is that where we pack our bags and say, "It's over between us, church. I'm going my way now." In a sense it's not that easy, and at once it's a million times easier.

It's not easy because still, way down deep in our souls, we harbor an awareness of that law we have violated. Like a stone thrown through the spider's web, the essence is left, but the threads are all tattered. We can carry guilt around like a bodybuilder and never make ourselves hard enough to hide the truth of our violation. But it's also a million times easier, for our God, who initiates this covenant of love and grace with us in the Old Testament, has never ceased to be a loving and gracious God. When Jesus went to the cross, and the veil of the temple rent in two, the threads in our hearts began to knit. As he instituted the Lord's Supper, Jesus passed the wine to his disciples and said, "'This cup is the new covenant in my blood, which is poured out for you'" (Luke 22:20). Instead of our bringing lambs or oxen to the altar, Jesus himself went there for us. That offering of the Son of God could occur only once and for all time. Through his blood, our relationship is sealed once and for all time.

Truly God is an elusive God. Like learning to swim in a mud puddle, my mind flails at the edges of knowing God. He is at once God above and beyond all things, one of such fierce majesty that to look upon his face is to die, and yet also God Immanuel, of such fierce tenderness that he walked among us men, women, and children and wore a crown of thorns that streaked his all-too-human face with blood. The picture slides. One seems to be the God I approach with the rational mind, all the catechisms and texts clutched to my chest as a kind of protection. Before the other I want to bow down and wash his dusty feet with my tears. Of one I am aware of the complete otherness; of the other I am aware of sorrows and grief, of laughter and tears.

One of the engineering marvels of the modern world is the bridge spanning the Straits of Mackinac, connecting Michigan's upper and lower peninsulas. "Mighty Mac" it is called, and no book I have read on it can possibly convey its might. It is the longest suspension bridge in the world; my younger son and I have often pored over pictures detailing its construction. The statistics are mind-boggling—so many cubic tons of concrete, so many thousands of miles of wire and cable. Armed with such information I think I know this bridge just a few hours' drive north of us.

Yet it isn't until I drive toward Mackinaw City, and first see those towers looming in the distance, and then feel the pavement beginning to lift upward to meet its height, and then feel the grid humming under the car's tires and flick side glances at sailboats and freighters far below, that I really *know* this bridge. It is when my knuckles turn white on the steering wheel and my heart lurches. Now I truly know its immensity. Now all the statistics make sense.

Similarly, our knowing God and our discovery of authentic faith lie in simply giving up our lives to him: I can't do it anymore, Lord. It's all yours. I don't understand this earthly situation any more than I can understand the engineering intricacies of some bridge. But I'll ride on it, and let you support me while I go.

CHAPTER 7

People of Fidelity

Reading: Nehemiah 1—2

Ezra's narrative ends with public confession by those who have sinned. Thereby the temple is also *spiritually* completed. An orderly structure for authentic faith has been set in place. Ezra will appear again in the narrative of Nehemiah, but first there is one more essential step in the rebuilding process to be completed.

Consider what we have seen in the process so far. The first task was the reconstruction of the altar. It marked a place—spiritually and physically—where the Israelites could take a stand in their sacred city. To all others in the area, the altar announced: "This is what we believe in, and the Lord of this sacred place is he in whom we believe." The altar was the spot where the Israelites could draw near to the heart of God and rekindle the first fires of their love for him.

The second step turned the Israelites toward the heap of broken rubble that had been the old temple. It had to be cleared out and begun anew. You can't begin a new work on old foundations. It won't last. New, solid foundations have to be constructed. Rocks hewn and perfectly sized have to be placed. It is almost as if this work will not only have to bear the weight of glory, but also secure it for a long time to come.

Then, and only then, could the temple be rebuilt. I imagine some of the Israelites just wanted to have a go at it. Use the old foundations, wait until the temple is done before erecting the altar—that sort of thing. We see where that would be wrong. The temple *could be* the most evident show of human achievement. It would be too easy to say, look what *we* have done for *our* God. No, the temple was the third step, built to solidify God's presence and authority in the midst of all the people. From the first block on the altar to the last step of the temple, this was God's work.

But it isn't finished. There is a final thing to do, no less important than the earlier steps. For the Israelites, as for us, boundaries are essential to protect the faith. Walls need to be rebuilt.

Fidelity and Fear

Today my wife and I took a thirteen-mile, end of summer bike ride around Reeds Lake and back home. It is a wonderful lake, just large enough to calm your spirit when you stop at the small park to rest before heading home. At its north end, the lake is spring-fed; at its south end it gets trapped in an algae-covered swampy area. Cattails hem the edges. Dead trees poke their long white trunks far over the watery muck. I remembered riding down there with my friends on summer afternoons when I was young. We'd plop our old fat-tire Schwinns by the side of the road and see how far into the swamp we could walk by balancing on fallen trees. Once, we made it to a decaying tree house still propped in upright arms. It was a miraculous thing to our young minds, a shrine to all those who had made their way there before. What daring to build such a tree house, thoroughly secluded, now a hidden monument to some earlier boys' bravery.

What struck me that afternoon, and what brought the scene back with such vivid recall (I almost believed I could see the point where we entered the swamp through the cattails), was the sudden sweet, musky odor of the swamp—rich and damp—which the breeze carried to us as we pedaled by. To me it was a fragrance rich with the spice of adventure, a joyful odor rising like an incense.

God's creation has always been a panorama of his glory. From the grand sweep of a range of mountains to the delicate grace of a single wildflower, this world declares the glory of God. And so should God's people, even when their skies darken and storms roll over the browned earth of their lives. Few of us escape those tests of our fidelity, those moments when we ourselves feel forsaken. Perhaps some of the following events in Nehemiah's life will help us understand what appears to be, at first glance, a conflict between our inner feelings that everything is going all wrong and the knowledge that our God reigns.

NEHEMIAH'S TEARS

In the year 456 BC, Nehemiah, who was in Persia, heard reports about the Jews who had returned to Jerusalem. At that time Ezra had been in Jerusalem about twelve years, and his work under God reestablished the temple. These new reports were troubling because the protective walls of the city had not yet been rebuilt. The gates still lay in ashes. Stones had tumbled down and left huge gaps in the wall. The threat to the temple was clear and present. The rejoicing contained at the close of Ezra's narrative gives way to mourning at the beginning of Nehemiah's narrative.

The transition from one narrative to another almost seems to symbolize the transitions in our own lives. So very few of us enjoy lives on a tranquil plain, moving smoothly and orderly from one event to another. On the contrary, the experience of the Christian life for many of us seems to be a random fluctuation where we question over and over, "Why this, Lord?" and try to discern his path in bleak and uneven places.

Where do you go then? Where did Nehemiah go? Down on his knees to begin: "When I heard these things, I sat down and wept" (1:4). Most of us who have scanned this story casually home in on Nehemiah's dramatic appearance before the king. But if we do so, we miss the most important part—Nehemiah's tears before God. Moreover, "For some days I mourned and fasted and prayed before the God of heaven" (1:4). No, he didn't run pell-mell to the king; he spent *days* in prayer before God. His actions formed a lamentation of spirit as he sought God.

Before anything else in this world—any relationship, any activity, any confrontation, or any new program—comes our fidelity to God. It is human nature to let our relationships or other events in this world preempt that. Our minds apprehend the problem that races to our emotions that react to the problem. All too often, the spiritual core of our being gets short-circuited: "What would God say about this? What would Jesus have us do?" Those are the essential first questions, and the questions we have to keep returning to in order to remain faithful. They should stand like huge flowing banners in our minds and hearts so that both are integrated with our spiritual allegiance to God.

Make a distinction here between the subject of the last

chapter and this one. To be a person of God, bearing an authentic faith is a matter of commitment. Authentic faith is an act of commitment to God. It declares that God is the final authority over my life and over all life. Fidelity is the act of living out that commitment in daily life. As with Nehemiah, the act of fidelity begins in prayer, seeking the Lord's leading in all matters. We pray in patience, remembering that Nehemiah spent days fasting and praying.

Nehemiah's prayer (1:5–11) has three precise parts. First, it is a prayer of confession. He confesses his own sins, but also intercedes for all his people (see vv. 5–7). As we have seen repeatedly in this study, confession is the necessary first step to approaching God.

Second, Nehemiah claims God's promises. Sometimes we are guilty of lifting our prayers like vague supplications. We fly our needs at half-mast in a windless sky. We have to learn, like Nehemiah in verses 8–9, to pray in boldness. Here he beseeches God to remember his promise to Moses: "If you are unfaithful, I will scatter you among the nations, but if you return to me and obey my commands, then even if your exiled people are at the farthest horizon, I will gather them from there and bring them to the place I have chosen as a dwelling for my Name." This is almighty God Nehemiah prays to, acknowledging that God has made never-failing promises.

Third, in verse 11, Nehemiah makes his petition. In effect, he says, "This is what I need, Lord." He asks God to bless the plan he has formed to meet with the king. Again, Nehemiah gives us an important pattern—to ask God's blessing upon work we are going to do and tasks we are going to undertake. In effect, Nehemiah remembers God's faithfulness in the past; now he implores God's very personal faithfulness in the fearful work he is about to do.

NEHEMIAH'S FEARS

Sometimes we spend so much time thinking about, planning for, and discussing our kingdom work that it doesn't even get started. Often church committees usurp individual initiative or, on the other hand, individuals initiate nothing because they believe the committees will do the work. Take a lesson from Nehemiah who had to act alone and under fearful circumstances to initiate the rebuilding of the walls. We can identify three distinct fears that Nehemiah had to overcome, each of which also bears profoundly on our own spiritual lives.

FEAR OF POWER

They were just a couple of common hoodlums. I see that now, looking back. But at the time I was only a fifth-grade safety at the school crossing, two blocks from home, two blocks from school. I had put on the bright orange-striped vest and placed the orange safety cone in the middle of the not very busy street.

I suppose it was a relief from boredom for them. It was terrifying to me.

They drove up in their car—I remember it was a black Mercury—and slowed ominously as they reached the intersection. There were no other cars in the street just then. The driver slowed and stopped right beside the cone. A cigarette dangled from his lip. "Hey, safety. What's this for?"

Suddenly my heart beat wildly. Sweat popped out under the vest. "That's for cars," I stammered. "This is a school crossing."

He spit the cigarette out and laughed. He reached out and grabbed the cone. Why weren't there any other cars? Why was I here, alone?

"Hey, safety. You want this back?" I stared at him. Terrified. Without words. Finally I shouted, "You can't do that!" With that the driver flung the orange cone across the street and drove off howling with laughter. I heard the mocking reply: "You can't do that!"

When I came home that afternoon, after seeing the "little kids" safely across the street, my heart was still beating hard, my hands still shaking. Maybe I was not very brave in fifth grade, but sometimes still my heart seems to jump in my throat and my hands tremble, and I find that I still have so few brave stories to tell.

It seems sometimes that our childhood fears stay with us the longest. Is it because they are the hardest to comprehend? Is it because then we know so little about evil and cruelty, that when they do occur they are driven like nails into our memories? Is it because we haven't developed the rational defenses ("just a couple of hoodlums") that carry us through adulthood? This much I have learned—if a person has fears, they are legitimate if only because they are fearful to that person.

Nehemiah's fear of the power of Artaxerxes was unquestionably legitimate. Truly, Nehemiah was in a favorable position. As cupbearer to the king, he was in a position of remarkable trust. Truly also, he had the king's confidence. That was necessary in the court during those days. Artaxerxes' own grandfather had been killed in his bedroom. A king couldn't be too careful with whom he surrounded himself.

But this appearance of Nehemiah would be altogether different. What Nehemiah had always shown to the king before was the outward face of the cheerful servant. That was his professional role. Nehemiah himself says that "I had not been sad in [Artaxerxes'] presence before" (2:1). No, he was the consummate professional butler. The moment of great risk and the deep fear lies in the fact that this time Nehemiah lets the mask slip and allows his personal feelings to surface above the professional role. The mourning that had been occurring in his heart now appears on his features. Artaxerxes perceives it. How will he interpret it? With anger? Mockery? The king asks Nehemiah, "Why does your face look so sad when you are not ill? This can be nothing but sadness of heart" (v. 2). Artaxerxes senses that the sadness lies deeper than physical illness.

What a risk of honesty Nehemiah took. As does any one of us who dares reveal our deepest need. The world says, "keep your feelings to yourself! They make life messy. We don't want to have to deal with that." Like Nehemiah in 2:2, we might say, "I was very much afraid." It is a dangerous, fearful thing to speak out of one's deepest need. Some of us don't even know whom to go to with it. Friendships are an increasingly rare commodity in this helter-skelter life of ours. What has crept in, like little rat's feet, is a haunting loneliness.

Nehemiah's first fear is that of revealing his true self. But, as he reports in 2:3, despite his fear, Nehemiah unburdened himself. His pain, he says, arises from the ruined walls of his sacred city.

FEAR OF THE RESPONSE

The first step for Nehemiah was to work up the sheer courage to reveal his inner self. However much afraid, Nehemiah blurts out his reasons: "Why should my face not look sad when the city where my fathers are buried lies in ruins, and its gates have been destroyed by fire?" (v. 3).

One can imagine that Artaxerxes is a bit perplexed. What thoughts flickered through his mind? So what do you want me to do about it? Or, listen, you're only my cupbearer. Don't bother me with your trivial problems. Remember that palace servants aren't even supposed to *have* feelings, much less show them. His is an honest perplexity. King Artaxerxes merely replies: "What is it you want?"

One can almost see Nehemiah take a deep breath, a gulp. Verse four tells us he "prayed to God in heaven," a quick, spontaneous prayer, just a heartbeat prayer really, before he answers. He requests nothing less than to be sent back to Jerusalem to rebuild the walls.

When the king seems to react favorably to the request, Nehemiah almost becomes brash in his requests. Nehemiah has good reason to press the issue. In a sense, he has a contract open before him and wants to close the deal. He asks for letters of safe conduct through the king's land. A wise request, for his caravan will be laden with treasures. He went even further, asking for a letter of permission to cut timber from the king's forests. All this the king granted, Nehemiah says, "because the gracious hand of my God was upon me" (2:8). Therein, of course, lies the answer. We commit our fears to the gracious hand of the Lord.

FEAR OF OPPOSITION AND RIDICULE

The private affairs are taken care of. Those fears of self-exposure and the response of others to it are done. Lurking in the area of Jerusalem, however, is a certain man named Sanballat the Horonite. Sanballat is simply described at this point as "very much disturbed that someone had come to promote the welfare of the Israelites" (2:10). Soon he will be doing his best to frustrate and ridicule that welfare. There always seems to be a Sanballat in our lives, someone quick to heap scorn and ridicule upon us, someone who takes pleasure in hindering our best efforts.

It's beside the point that opposition and ridicule are themselves often ridiculous. The important thing is how we react to the ridicule of others. There will always be those Sanballats who just don't like us for who we are and who want to get in the way of what we do. And Sanballat wasn't about to just let Nehemiah alone. Why should we expect otherwise? Whenever we engage in the work of God we can expect opposition. Jesus made it clear to us: "If the world hates you, keep in mind that it hated me first. If you belonged to the world, it would love you as its own. As it is, you do not belong to the world, but I have chosen you out of the world. That is why the world hates you" (John 15:18–19). The effort of Nehemiah was nothing less than to rescue the sacred city out of the world. Sanballat would be around—as Sanballats are always around today—to ridicule and frustrate that labor.

As a college teacher, almost daily I have to deal with the fears of young adults. I sometimes come home amazed and exhausted with the range of individual concerns that pop up in the course of a day. They extend, at one end of the scale, with students requesting not to be called on in class because they're too shy or anxious or uncertain of their own abilities. Since my courses rely heavily on discussion, I have to keep a careful eye on those unable to participate. Along with that group, several students may have learning disabilities and request certain testing procedures and the like. All such fears and needs are legitimate. I honor them professionally and discreetly.

Other fears are harder to deal with. Jodi (not her actual name) came in to see me about an essay she was writing. Within five minutes, as the tissue box on my conference table emptied, it was perfectly obvious that Jodi's essay was not her foremost need. Carrying nearly a straight-A average in her course work, she was terribly undecided, in her junior year, what major to pursue and what career to follow. That was only part of the story.

When Jodi was a young girl, her parents had divorced. Jodi had grown up on their farm, four hundred acres of barely productive, southern Michigan sandy soil. It was always too wet or too dry. Because of the poor soil, her father was seldom able to pay support to Jodi and her mother. Yet she remembered as some of her happiest days working during the summer on the farm. Always cruelly pinched for money, Jodi was making her way through college on scholarships, some loans, and her meager earnings from a part-time job.

As I listened, especially during the long silences when she dabbed at her eyes with tissues, I thought I sensed her needs. One was financial, surely. But how did that translate into a career choice? With her brilliant academic record, Jodi could pretty much select any career (and financial security) that she wanted. But the deeper need was obviously the disastrous effects upon her of that bitter divorce. Her greatest sadness was the fact that her father was not a Christian, that he had ignored her for years, and that she longed for some reconciliation.

Although I continued to see Jodi (she took four courses with me), she needed far more directed counseling than I could give her. I arranged professional counseling for her, but stayed in close touch with her.

As it turned out, Jodi's career selection spoke to her first love. After graduation she apprenticed for two years on organic farms and is now managing her own organic farm. But before she graduated, she also met with her father. As a Christian, she said, she had to forgive him and express her love for him. "That was all I could do," she wrote me, "even though I was terrified to do it. No, there wasn't any sudden change in him, but now I have hope."

Our deepest needs also have to be answered deep within. If Jodi had selected any other career, it would have been a balm, but not healing. Farming was and is the deep call on her life. If Jodi had not worked up the courage to face her fear and talk with her father, she would not have had the spiritual peace she now possesses. We still, from moment to moment, act out the sadness and fear of Nehemiah on our journey to renewal and joy.

But as Nehemiah knew, and as Jesus taught us, we don't always meet with joy in this life. Too often we confront the hatred of the world that Jesus spoke of. Here another example from my profession intrudes painfully on my memory.

My first full-time teaching position was at a Christian liberal arts college in the eastern United States. That description is misleading. For years the college had slipped steadily into the pit of modernism. Its Christian foundation became nothing more than a slogan, and one as hollow as an abandoned church. Atheists now spoke to the students, most of them openly derisive of Christian faith. It was one of the most beautiful campuses I have ever walked on, and one seething with discord.

The board of trustees hired a new president, a man of national reputation and sterling credentials, and charged him with restoring the spiritual foundations of the college. Further, they gave him a mandate to hire as many young Christian scholars as he could in order to turn the program around. I was one of those hired under that charge. What followed were several years of the most challenging, exhilarating, and exhausting work I have ever done.

But the pockets of resistance didn't disappear overnight. Nearly every day someone in this growing group of Christian teachers was called upon to defend the faith and the idea of a Christian college. Exchanges in the coffeehouse grew heated. It was hard to maintain the calm of reason that we had committed ourselves to. But slowly the situation changed. Where once people had gathered in dark rooms, lit by shifting candles, to hold séances and commune with evil spirits, students and faculty now gathered for prayer vigils or praise singing.

When Indira (not her actual name) first came to see me, I was surprised. I knew that, even though she had lived in the States for several years now, she still clung tenaciously to the Hindu gods of her native India. A young woman of startling beauty and a quick mind, she spoke often in classes and groups on the virtue and superiority of Hinduism. I was very surprised, then, when she came by my office to talk about Christianity.

We met twice. While she questioned many of the things I said, she seemed genuinely interested.

The third time we met was quite different. About midway through our discussion, I noticed her face contorting. She couldn't respond when I asked her a question. Her lips flared back as if in a grimace of pain. I fought off a shiver of apprehension. Suddenly she bolted upright and stood rigidly before my desk. Her eyes seemed frozen at some point past my shoulder. Her rigid lips cracked, and a sound, more like a deep animal growl than any human voice, came from her.

"I hate you," the voice snarled. "I hate you. And I hate your God!"

It seemed that her body collapsed around her and she rushed from the room. I bent my head and prayed, oblivious to the open door and people walking past in the hallway. Miraculously, the icicles in my heart thawed. I had never witnessed such pure and violent hatred. I never saw her again during those last few weeks until her graduation.

Such examples reveal to me that the challenges of Nehemiah, his tears and his fears, are still very much with us today. Jesus' words ring profoundly, "If the world hates you, keep in mind that it hated me first." Yes, but since the world hated Jesus *first*, he enacted the victory over evil that delivers us from hatred *today*. Just as God delivered Nehemiah, leading him to safety when he acted on his belief, so God acts on our behalf when we place our trust in him. The gates of hell and all its demons shall not prevail against us (see Matt. 16:18).

Faith and fidelity are delicately interwoven in the Christian life, yet one is built upon the other—stones upon the foundation. Authentic faith recognizes the absolute authority and order of God, and our relationship with him. That is the foundation.

Fidelity, on the other hand, brings our faith to the world in actions. We see from Nehemiah that fidelity to God is never a matter of quietly withdrawing from the world, just turning it over to the Sanballats to corrupt as they please. That is our temptation—and our downfall if we give in to it. We can't pretend that we can retire to the quiet sanctuaries of our churches and that the world "out there" no longer exists. It does, and it's going to hell with locomotive speed. It's on a runaway course. Keeping fidelity to God requires us to get out there, to take control of the locomotive, to get in the cab if we can. So often we ask, "What would Jesus do?" We already have the answer. Here's what Jesus did. He turned the temple of his time on its established gray head. He went out to the dangerous byways. He ate with sinners. He brought love to the unlovely. He brought hope to the hopeless. Keeping fidelity is like signing a document promising to walk in that way. Through his tears, and in spite of his fears, Nehemiah gives us lessons in just how to do this— even when it is very dangerous.

CHAPTER 8

Preparing for Action

Reading: Nehemiah 3—5

ॐ

Whenever Nehemiah arrived in Jerusalem, the external threat doubled, then tripled. Sanballat, the governor of Samaria, was joined by Tobiah the Ammonite. Later their confederacy would expand further as Geshem, in charge of a vast territory from Egypt to southern Palestine, joined them. In the middle stood Nehemiah, with a band of priests and laborers he had inherited from Zerubbabel. Not good odds. It is little wonder that upon his arrival in Jerusalem Nehemiah inspected the walls under cover of darkness. He knew from the outset that danger rather than security surrounded him.

The following morning he revealed his plans to the community leaders. They quickly agreed and set to work (Neh. 2:18). But there he was again. The eager-eyed Sanballat, along with Tobiah and Geshem, "mocked and ridiculed us" (v. 19). Still the wall rose, section by section, gate by gate. As it rose under the leadership of the priests, the enemy's ridicule deepened to anger. The mockery intensified. Here's Tobiah's taunt: "What they are building—if even a fox climbed up on it, he would break down their wall of stones" (4:3). Thus far the Israelites had not been attacked, but—as can sometimes be even worse—they were despised. Being despised eats at a person's spirit and purpose. It also can gnaw at the core of one's faith.

We sometimes wonder why it is that, when we try hard to do right by the Lord, things can still go so badly. Like Nehemiah, we plead, "Hear us, O our God, for we are despised" (v. 4). And, frankly, the most common attitude toward Christians by the secular world today is spite—we are the subject of mockery and laughter. How on earth can we dare to keep our faith in action? Nehemiah gives us several very direct and forceful answers.

POSTING A GUARD

Nehemiah wielded a physical sword, because his enemies were physical. They feared the rise of Jerusalem as a Middle Eastern power once again; no doubt they remembered when Israel subdued the whole land. Now it seemed very likely that Sanballat's combined forces might launch a preemptive strike against Jerusalem. Nehemiah's response was this: "We prayed to our God and posted a guard day and night to meet this threat" (v. 9). That second clause in particular is important. Our enemies may not be like Nehemiah's, but the threat is still such that we have to post a guard day and night.

A recovering alcoholic cannot say, "I'll abstain during the day, but have only one drink after dinner." The pornography addict cannot say, "I'll cruise the Internet porno sites only on weekends, and thereby keep it under control." Similarly, if someone develops a flirtatious relationship with, say, a co-worker or office mate, but thinks that it's just good sporting fun and won't go anywhere because they both head to their own homes at night, he's wrong. There's trouble at the walls of their lives, and they had better do what Nehemiah did: pray to God and be on guard night and day.

We have to append a footnote here. Nehemiah just didn't have all that many people in and around Jerusalem. He was surrounded on all sides with incomplete boundaries standing between them and the enemy. The Israelites seemed as vulnerable as bugs under an elephant's footfalls. Where does such courage come from?

First of all, Nehemiah met the threat practically and head-on. At the most broken areas of the walls he stationed guards and soldiers. He recognized the weaknesses of the wall and *attacked them* with sure defenses. Similarly, we have to locate the weaknesses in our lives and rush spiritual aid to that point. If the traveling sales rep is most vulnerable to pornography in the lonely, late-night hours at the motel room, he has to consider in advance how to occupy those hours. Cut off the enemy before he can creep in.

Second, however, Nehemiah breathed powerful encouragement into the workers: "Don't be afraid of them. Remember the LORD who is great and awesome, and fight for your brothers, your sons and your daughters, your wives and your homes" (v. 14). As we have seen earlier, this is a prevailing theme in Scripture: Our courage comes from the Lord, not from ourselves. Curiously, however, when we look at that theme in Scripture, we see that it is the precise counterpart to worldly measures, which take courage from numbers of soldiers and the power of weaponry. So it has always been.

Consider Gideon. Judges 6 tells how the powerful Midianites had struck such fear into the Israelites that the people had retreated to caves and hollows in the mountainous wilderness. In the midst of this desolation, an angel

appeared to Gideon and said, "The LORD is with you" (v. 12).
Gideon gave exactly the response I would have given: "If
the Lord is with us, why has all this happened to us? Where
are all his wonders that our fathers told us about?" (v. 13).
There's the oldest question in history again: "Why me,
Lord? Where are you when I need you? What am I doing
living in this cave while the Midianites are walking off with
my grain and livestock?"

This is a young, inexperienced Gideon here, not the war-
rior of God he is remembered for in his later years. At this
stage, he's pretty much a coward. Several times he protests
his weakness. Each time the Lord answers him: "I will be
with you" (6:16). It took a long time and a long road for
Gideon to find courage. Remarkably, however, these passages show us God's patience even with a reluctant follower.
He permits our human cowardice to mature into spiritual
courage. The important thing is that Gideon did act and
defeated the Midianites as God had promised.

The powerful and oft-repeated theme in Scripture is simply this: Few are many when God is with them. We see the
theme enacted when the Israelites, as recorded in I Samuel
14, were again hiding in wilderness dens for fear of the
Philistines. In an incredibly gutsy move, Jonathan and his
young armor bearer have a go at the Philistines. Why?
Where does the courage come from? Here's what Jonathan
says, "Nothing can hinder the LORD from saving, whether by
many or by few" (v. 6). Jonathan's act of courage, moreover,
gives courage to others. It's infectious. The Israelites crawl
out of their dens. As Jonathan wades into battle—with only
his armor bearer!—the Israelites start surging behind him. It
only took one man of courage, one man who believed that
little is much when the Lord is with them, to turn fear into
conviction.

So it was for Nehemiah. He breathed courage into the few so that they would not run away but stand guard. They could be depended upon now. This whole matter of posting a guard is a matter of dependability, and so often it takes only that one person of courage to fortify not just the gates but the spirits of the people.

It is not only Gideon, or Jonathan, or Nehemiah to whom we look as models. This idea of having the courage to post a strong guard because the few are many when the Lord is with them runs throughout Scripture. We could multiply examples. How about Ruth, with her incredible courage to follow Naomi? And surely, we eventually have to turn to a distant descendant of Ruth. We have to turn to that lowliest of births in Bethlehem. We have to turn to the least of humanity, a baby, for our courage and inspiration to stand guard. Here indeed the few are many when the Lord is with them, because the infinite God took on the incarnate form of humanity. Jesus, who once was least, is now our risen Lord. So we stand guard, often feeling lonely and insufficient, but trying to take courage nonetheless on the certain knowledge that Jesus reigns and will return again.

"But," you might say, "God acted directly in response to his people during those dim reaches of history. I don't find it hard to believe that God encouraged Gideon. What about today? I don't seem to hear his voice." Two important truths apply here. First, God is the Lord of *all* history, not just a few thousand years before Christ. Our history has changed unbelievably; God's nature is unchanging and believable through all history. In his classic work *Knowing God*, J. I. Packer targets the issue:

> For the God with whom they [biblical persons] had to do is the God with whom we have to do.

> We could sharpen the point by saying, *exactly* the
> same God; for God does not change in the least
> particular. Thus it appears that the truth on
> which we must dwell in order to dispel this feel-
> ing that there is an unbridgeable gulf between
> men in Bible times and our own, is the truth of
> God's *immutability*. (68)

We see, first, that God himself doesn't change. Second, however, we recognize the different ways that God speaks to us today. As we emphasized in an earlier chapter, one such way is through the church and the preaching of God's Word. Another way is through prayer, both individual and corporate. Yet another way arises from small group studies where we receive the prayerful direction of others.

Those of us who have served in the armed forces know the importance of keeping guard. It starts from the first moment of basic training with "fire guard." The directions for and tests in keeping guard never let up. I'm sure that others can recall shivering through a pouring rain in the middle of the night, fighting to stay awake. Or having an officer suddenly appear at some early morning hour and quiz you on something like "fire safety" or the salient configurations of an M-16 rifle. Or spending nights deep in the hard clay of Vietnam, and hoping the clay is hard enough.

Nehemiah knew about keeping guard. If we're going to repair the gaps in the wall, we had better post a strong guard while the process is under way. Nehemiah made a strategic defense. Half the men would stand guard, heavily armed, prepared to do battle at a moment's notice. But only half the men. Nehemiah's purpose was not to wait around for some battle; it was to rebuild the wall. Therefore the other half kept to that task.

Notice a strategic division also among these. The skilled craftsmen, doing the actual work on the wall, also had swords by their sides so they could work as quickly and efficiently as possible. Those carrying the materials for the wall—rocks and mortar and gravel packing and whatever else was necessary—actually held the sword in one hand and the material in the other. Nehemiah created a perfect symbiosis of keeping guard under the sword and working to protect the sacred city. Like well-appointed currents in a stream, the differing teams merged into one living organism.

A FIGHT PLAN AT THE GAPS

Perhaps the very worst fight plan would be a random action in response to attacks of oppression. We need a unifying strategy. Henry Cloud developed one such strategy in his book, *Changes That Heal*. Cloud shows how one can make a transition from past events, particularly those bearing psychological and spiritual damage, to a renewal of self for the future. The key is to set boundaries, both in one's sense of selfhood and in the actions one commits. If we have to place ourselves near or in any such situation where our walls are weak, we have to develop a spiritual fight plan as effective as Nehemiah's to guard those gaps. Each of us has to name his or her own weak points in order to protect ourselves.

Cloud points out that this action of defining boundaries both separates us from an old self and guides the discovery of a renewed self. He puts it like this: "When we think of boundaries, we think of the limits. Boundaries give us a sense of what is part of us and what is not part of us, what we will allow and what we won't, what we will choose to do and what we will choose not to do" (95). As with the Israelites, walls exist to keep the enemy out and the people safe within. They are the demarcations between safety and danger that one must recognize and never cross.

Unfortunately, the effort for most of us is more complicated than merely *choosing* to do or not to do something. In addition to boundaries, then, we must also establish clear goals.

To fight may be understood not only in a negative sense but also positively. The negative sense of the word declares—this is the enemy. These are the limits beyond which I will not go, and within which I will not let the enemy enter." We cannot be responsible for every thought, every temptation that enters our thought life. But when contrary and deceptive ones do, we can exercise the authority of 2 Corinthians 10:5, "We take captive every thought to make it obedient to Christ." That is the action—the warfare, if you will—of the fight plan, but we also have to ask to what goal it is directed. Where does it lead? Are we endlessly skirmishing on the plains, feeling the drumbeats, and ringing of weapons relentlessly in our minds?

To establish limits without goals simply intensifies the crisis of temptation. We can expend our spiritual energies, ceaselessly struggling over wrongful and self-indulgent pleasures and relentlessly reflecting upon such events, past and present. The goal, however, is freedom. We want to be free of the guilt and spiritual lostness. We also want to be freed from the *need* for battle and freed for some sense of comfort and security in daily living.

This stage of action is like a rational decision we force upon the emotional resistance. It is grounded in this: "If the Son sets you free, you will be free indeed." Those are Jesus' words in John 8:36. Freedom is Jesus' fundamental message, and in the specific context of the John 8 discourse it is freedom *from* sin *to* life eternal. The first step in the freedom phase of the fight plan, then, is declaration of the facts: I am freed in Jesus Christ.

Furthermore, it is vital to nourish that declaration with the support of others. Having been freed *from*, we need help in being freed *to*. This too is part of the fight plan. Besides my wife, my family, my friends and church, I rely heavily upon a group of men for accountability and support. Founded on the inviolable premise of complete confidentiality, upon the necessity of bringing individual needs before God in regular devotions, and careful study of God's Word for direction in our lives, this group formed a core of friendship and understanding, of laughter and tears, of confession and forgiveness.

Some people might argue that they would never "open up" in a small group. In some cases, as Charles Whitfield has pointed out in *Healing the Child Within*, it is best not to. He observes:

> When we share our feelings, it is most appropriate to do so with safe and supportive people.
> Early in recovery people who grew up in troubled or dysfunctional families may want so much to share that they get rejected, betrayed or otherwise get into trouble by telling others, indiscriminately, about their feelings. They may find it difficult to learn that it is *not appropriate to share feelings with everyone* [emphasis mine]. (82)

It is essential, Whitfield writes, to check disclosure against the responses of others. If, for example, they are more interested in giving advice than in listening or asking questions, it is probably not a "safe" group.

Nonetheless, a safe support group is important, perhaps even essential, for spiritual growth. It may take time to find one; it may even require starting one. Often, the gaps in our own walls rob us of a sense of self-worth, of value in a larger community, of goals for "freed" living. Hence the need for a unity with others to grow in new directions. In a discussion of the bonding process with others, Henry Cloud points out that we "attack" in order to separate:

> Bonding is first and foremost a stage to growth.
> We must be able to have relationships with oth-
> ers to be alive. This is the unity that underlies
> the relational aspects of the image of God.
> (*Changes,* 115)

If someone cannot attack, separateness has no meaning. It is a no without a yes. We must be able to be "a part" of someone or something before we can be "apart." Attachment gives us the safety and the strength to separate from the past. In this respect, then, the support group functions as a place of safety as one fights against the past and searches for the freedom to find new patterns of living.

As stated earlier, Nehemiah wielded a literal sword because his enemies were physical. We, however, do battle, as Paul wrote, against powers and principalities. These include all the deceitful allurements of this world and the temptations of Satan—all those things ready to creep on their clawed feet through the gaps in our walls. But Paul also tells us how to stand guard against them. In Ephesians 6:10–18, Paul cautions us to put on the "whole armor of God" (v. 11). He is a spiritual realist and uses very concrete figures to describe the warfare with evil. The final, and perhaps most important armament is "the sword of the Spirit, which is the word of God" (v. 17). The idea is also central in the epistle to the Hebrews, where the writer insists that "The word of God is living and active. Sharper than any double-edged sword" (4:12). That is our equivalent to the swords Nehemiah's men carried.

If we are seriously going to pursue faith in action, we need to know the Bible. Sadly, biblical ignorance is the tragic failure of modern Christendom. Scorned by the world, the words of wisdom have been reduced to whispers. In complete frustration after a class session, one of my colleagues said to me, "These students couldn't find Genesis in the Bible if they started at the beginning." Hyperbole surely. But the very point of hyperbole is to expose some underlying truth. The truth here is that we have to let the Word of God so saturate us through memorization and study—we have to "eat" the Word as someone has put it—that it becomes a part of our very nature. It is our task to put muscular definition on the Word in our lives.

Faith in action is a hard exercise, as daunting as any five-mile run. Sharpening the sword of the Spirit, or letting Scripture harden like trained muscles at the center of one's life, takes hard work. It requires preparation and relentless workouts. Why? Because as Sanballat prowled the gaps in the wall that Nehemiah desperately worked to rebuild, Satan probes just as hard for gaps in our defenses.

CHAPTER 9

People of Action

Reading: Matthew 25:31–46

The first two steps of faith in action seem perfectly reasonable. First, we have to post a strong guard. This is not a passive defense but an active one, alert to every threat. We put it in intimately personal terms. If we find ourselves attracted to a particular temptation, we must post a strong, active plan of defense that guards against it. Second, we have to seize the courage to wield the sword of the Word of God. Where does such courage come from? From the sure conviction that few are many when the Lord is with them. This sounds like a battle plan. It was for Nehemiah; it is for us.

SOCIAL JUSTICE

As God has assured our survival, so we must also ensure the survival of others. A dominant theme of the Old Testament is that God lives among, loves, and aids his faithful people. It reaches a climax in the New Testament in the incarnation of God's love in Jesus. Why did God bother with this miracle of the incarnation? The answer was given by Jesus himself: "For

God so loved the world that he gave his one and only Son, that whoever believes in him shall not perish but have eternal life" (John 3:16).

A powerful secondary theme runs parallel to this throughout Scripture. Because God has given us life, we protect and nurture the lives of others. The two are inextricably and eternally bound.

There is really only one good reason why a Christian must fully engage in social justice. It is not first of all a matter of voting with a Christian conscience, although that is part of it. Nor is it first of all a matter of trying to alleviate the scourge of hunger, or a myriad of other needs that tug upon our hearts. First of all, above all, we engage in social justice because Jesus told us to do so. And he didn't just tell us once; he told us over and over again, summarizing it most powerfully in his commandment: "Love one another. As I have loved you, so you must love one another. By this all men will know that you are my disciples, if you love one another" (John 13:34–35). While Jesus commanded his disciples to love one another, he made it perfectly clear in his own life and actions that his heart of love was not limited to those nearest and dearest. It extended to the unlovely and unlovable.

At one point Jesus was asked a tricky question. One of the keepers of the Law, a Pharisee, asked Jesus what the greatest commandment was. Jesus properly responded with the very familiar words taken from Deuteronomy 6:5: "'Love the Lord your God with all your heart and with all your soul and with all your mind.' This is the first and greatest commandment" (Matt. 22:37–38). But then immediately, Jesus added the lesser known words from Leviticus 19:18: "And the second is like it: 'Love your neighbor as yourself'" (Matt. 22:39). It is fair to say that, in his teachings and actions, Jesus' whole life on earth was all about *showing* how those two great command-ments mesh. To love God *is* to love your neighbor.

Furthermore, when we think about social justice, we do well to remember Jesus' attitude toward the whole world. In his magnificent discourse with Nicodemus, recorded in John 3:1–21, Jesus made clear the purpose of his presence on earth. God gave his one and only Son. Why? "So that *whoever* believes in him shall not perish but have eternal life" (v. 16, emphasis mine). Moreover, Jesus makes clear that his task is not to condemn the world but to save it (see vv. 16–18). Often we read those familiar words all too quickly. As we linger over them, we can't help being impressed by Jesus' extravagant love for the world. Looking out upon the world, we think to our-selves: These are the people Jesus loves! Here, that man rolled in the sleeping bag, stinking of urine and sweat, who will tell him how much Jesus loves him? Who will, like the good Samaritan of Jesus' parable, lift him off the street?

The very first, and constantly foremost, reason we are compelled to enact social justice, then, is because Jesus com-manded us to. I like the way Thomas Kelly puts it in *A Testament of Devotion*:

> "As the father hath sent me, even so send I you"
> becomes, not an external, Biblically authorized
> command, but a living, burning experience. For
> the experience of an inflooding, all-enfolding
> Love, which is at the center of Divine Presence, is
> of a Love which *embraces all creation*, not just our
> little, petty selves [emphasis mine]. (89)

That inward burning is nothing less than the work of the Holy Spirit, nudging us to be Christ's heart, hands, and feet in a suffering world.

Necessarily, Jesus makes clear, the vertical relationship

between humans and the transcendent God will be demonstrated horizontally from person to person. The horizontal relationships—our care for others in spiritual and physical need—directly mirror our vertical relationship. If we are not caring for the needy, there is something deeply wrong between us and our God.

The Christian's idea of neighborly love and social action is a matter of faith and also ethics. This is how we ought to live given our relationship with God. In his important work *Reason Within the Bounds of Religion,* Nicholas Wolterstorff points out that "committing yourself to be a Christ-follower also presupposes that you have some conviction about the complex of action and belief that your following of Christ *ought* to be realized in.... The complex of action and belief that its realization *ought* in fact to assume, for any given person, is what I shall call his *authentic* Christian commitment" (68). We may ask what such actions are that authenticate our faith in Jesus. They are precisely those that model his behavior when he walked here as a human being on this earth. That, as I have discovered, can be hard to do.

Reuben Johnson showed up at my side door on one of the hottest days of August. The sun boiled in a sky empty of clouds. As if heaven held its breath, no breeze stirred. Leaves on the trees drooped like a lolling dog's tongue. And Reuben Johnson was hungry.

I didn't know what to make of him. He was about my height—six feet three—weighed about 275 pounds, and had a scar that bisected his left cheek. The entire length of him dripped with sweat. His eyes had a reddish tinge, as if some fire burned behind them. This Reuben Johnson wasn't any teddy bear.

I offered to give him a dollar for bus fare to the mission. That wasn't what Reuben had in mind.

"Naw. That ain't right," he said, shaking his ponderous head. His head was shaved and gleamed slick with sweat as if under a sheen of oil. "Man tol' me you was an elder."

True. I was an elder. About ten years earlier.

"What man was this?"

"Man uppa corner. By the church. I needs some food. Been walkin' all day."

My wife Pat was listening through the screen door. She poked her head out. "I can heat up some food for you," she said.

Yikes! I was about to go in and close the door. But not now. I walked out to the porch with Reuben Johnson while Pat layered slabs of leftover ham, a derrick load of potatoes, and string beans onto a plate and squeezed it into the microwave.

Reuben was agitated. He sat on the porch step kneading hands as thick as catchers' mitts. "Walkin' all day," he said. "Lookin' for work. Stoppin' in every store."

"You live around here?" I asked.

"Naw. Come here to get a job. Ruby's here. Gotta find Ruby."

"Ruby?"

"My ex. Divorced me when I went to Jackson."

Jackson? The state penitentiary?

"When was that?" I asked.

"Seven years ago. Just got out on parole yesterday. Lookin' for a job all day. Just walkin'. Nobody wants to hire me."

"You know," I offered hopefully, "folks at the mission can help you find work. Maybe I can take you there."

Anything to get you off my porch step, I was thinking.

"No!" he shouted. "Can't get a job. I tell 'em my record, say I was in for murder, they don't wanna hear nothing."

He was fidgeting ponderously now, shifting his weight. I was paralyzed.

"Murder. Wasn't even my fault. Came at me with a knife. See this?" He pointed to his cheek. What was I supposed to say? The scar snaked down his cheek in a livid ridge. Oh, I didn't notice?

"I took the knife right out of his hand and killed him with it. That's why I only got ten years. Out in seven. Now I got no job, no money. Ruby'll hep me. Better hep me."

Pat came out with a steaming tray. Deftly she slipped a twenty-dollar bill into Reuben's hand when she handed him the tray. His eyes were huge.

"I think we should pray first," she said. And we did, there on the step to the back porch.

The food disappeared in a flash, followed by two huge glasses of milk. He sighed deeply, belched gently—like an elephant with a head cold.

I asked him if he knew where Ruby lived. "Got an address on some paper," he said. He fished around in his pocket, found the paper, read the address.

Oh no, I thought. I don't want to go down *there*.

It was getting dark. The buses had stopped running. Reuben had been walking all day.

"Would you like me to take you to Ruby's?" I asked.

I kept the air conditioning howling at full blast all the way to Ruby's house. Still, his hand was wet with sweat when we arrived. He held it out to shake. I squeezed it and wished him well.

"Thank the Missus again for the food," he said, "and the prayer."

I confess that I had had no interest in being a neighbor to Reuben. Then there he was on my porch, big and sweaty and unavoidable. Hard to spot the image of God in him. But

I don't think he could have spotted it in me either. If not for the kind intervention of Pat, I probably would have made my way to the phone to call the police. I needed a Nehemiah lesson.

Nehemiah and Social Justice

Nehemiah's struggle to complete the wall continued. Apparently all the able-bodied men, both from inside the city and also from outlying homesteads, were called upon to participate. Not only were provisions needed for these men, but also their personal work was left untended, cutting off their family income. Moreover, grain was in short supply because of a famine in the land. People were literally going unfed. To make ends meet, they had taken out loans from wealthier Jews, who charged them a large amount of interest (usury) on the loans—a practice forbidden for needy people in the Old Testament (see Ex. 22:25; Deut. 15:7–8; 23:19).

Most commentators point out that the events of Nehemiah 5 actually take place after the rebuilding of the wall, rather than in the midst of it as suggested by its placement in our Scripture. They argue that it is unlikely that Nehemiah would have called the large public meeting that he did during the feverish activity of building. That may be, but the work on the wall precipitated the crisis. More than one of those workers was wondering something like this: Here I am, supposedly doing the Lord's work. And my family is going hungry. What's going wrong here? And with this famine, I have little hope of growing enough grain to pay back my loans. Will someone please stand up and give me some answers?

Nehemiah will, and his discourse points out the necessity of faith in action for social justice. In colloquial terms, here's where the rubber meets the road. This is where your faith is challenged. Are you ready to put it into action, or are you just going to sit on your hands?

Nehemiah's address to his people follows several interesting steps. He reminds them that they had brought back their kinsmen from bondage to Gentiles—the Babylonians and Assyrians. Now, in order to secure their debts or to finance the high interest charges, these same Jews are having to post their sons or daughters as collateral. Basically, nothing has changed. Instead of being enslaved to foreigners, they are enslaved to their kinsmen. The fact infuriates Nehemiah and causes him to call the group meeting.

More than his personal anger lies behind this discourse, however. What is happening here violates a fundamental premise of Jewish society and God's law for social justice. For example, in past history a Jewish worker who fell into debt could place himself into service to another person to pay off that debt (see Lev. 25:39–40). But under the rules of Jubilee, he would be freed in the seventh year (see Deut. 15:12–18). Now the debt-struck persons were forced to put up their own children as collateral, with little hope of freedom unless the debts were paid. This situation more nearly imitates those people who took the Israelites into bondage, yet it was being practiced by their kinsmen.

One can look to history to understand Nehemiah's anger, but one can also look to other events of his time. As the nation had fallen into moral dissolution under a reeling cycle of profligate kings, prophets such as Amos tried desperately to call them back to first things. True, Amos prophesied nearly three hundred years before the events of Nehemiah, but his message was so thoroughly grounded in a common biblical theme, and so pervasive in the Jewish sacred texts, that it serves as a foundation for all their and our dealings with others. We are, Amos reminds us, children of God. If that is so, then we are to deal with others as if dealing with God himself. That is a staggering approach to social justice— so simple in concept but so overpowering in its demands. Here's what Amos said in God's name:

> I hate, I despise your religious feasts; I cannot
>   stand your assemblies.
> Even though you bring me burnt offerings and
>   grain offerings, I will not accept them.
> Though you bring choice fellowship offerings, I
>   will have no regard for them.
> Away with the noise of your songs!
>   I will not listen to the music of your harps.
> But let justice roll on like a river, righteousness
>   like a never-failing stream! (Amos 5:21–24)

For Amos, one's faith necessarily must be enacted in deeds of social justice.

That's what Amos prophesied. Here's what Nehemiah does. In the assembly of the people, Nehemiah denounces the actions of the people. Moreover, he takes the lead in setting things straight. He lends his money without charging any interest to those in need. He calls upon others to give back the money they have acquired by their loans. Incredibly, they agree to do so. As a symbol of their pact, Nehemiah takes off his robe, shakes it, and proclaims, "In this way may God shake out of his house and possessions every man who does not keep this promise" (Neh. 5:13). That was the most powerful statement of the day. As we deal with others, so too we deal with the God who made them.

Social justice is predicated upon the belief that we are to treat others precisely as they are, persons created by almighty God. We are to do this not just to the lovely, the friendly, the well-to-do; we are to do it also to the unlovely and unloved, to those who would harm us, and to those who are dying of destitution. We are to do it for those who have never heard that they are children of God, and for those who deny God. We are to do it for them because God did it for us.

There is a step beyond Amos and beyond Nehemiah, however. It is the step that Jesus walked. In his discourse on the living bread recorded in John 6, Jesus pointed out, "I have come down from heaven not to do my will but to do the will of him who sent me. And this is the will of him who sent me, that I shall lose none of all that he has given me, but raise them up at the last day" (vv. 38–39). And who is included in that "all"? Surely not the Pharisees alone, who, Jesus said, would be judged by the very law they practiced. Nor even the disciples alone, those profoundly perplexed followers who sometimes wondered just who it was that they followed. No, that "all" included people like Mary Magdalene, the outcast from society. It included ragged village children who played with Jesus. It included the social outcasts, the misfits who wouldn't know what social justice meant if a band of philosophers tried to teach them. The only way these outcasts and misfits learned was through Jesus' action. They were touched in all their destitution and unloveliness; that touch brought them the riches of eternal life and the love of God.

It came with a price, nonetheless. Perhaps we have become too at ease with our financial exercise of social justice. It is safe and easy to donate x amount of dollars to the local mission to feed the homeless in the inner city. It is hard and sometimes dangerous to participate in the mission program yourself. But faith in action puts the person ahead of the dollars. Always. And for a simple reason. The price of our salvation has already been paid, brutally so, when Jesus took that step to the cross and bought our freedom.

This work of putting faith into action can be a fearful enterprise. We doubt our courage. We feel we don't have experience. We don't trust our words. We are too mindful of our own sin to try to minister to others. All these things are true. No one claims this work is easy. But we are the redeemed people of God, his chosen ones (see 1 Peter 2:9). And like Nehemiah we must post a close guard around our lives; we must always remain alert to the attacks of Satan and those whispers of deceit he breathes in our ears. Like Nehemiah we must grasp the sword of the Spirit, ready to defend our position of truth or to go forth to establish it further. Lastly, like Nehemiah we must work toward social justice. In doing so, however, we have a perfect model—our Savior himself.

CHAPTER 10

Connections with the Lord of History

Reading: Jeremiah 33

It was a swampy day in Mississippi. Sunday morning. The sun rose like a huge red flame above the fields. Mist still hovered over the ground, like fog rolling at eye level. Rain had splattered the earth off and on for a week, saturating the loamy soil.

Sunday morning. The clapboard church rose atop a block foundation. Its whitewashed boards were stripped by wind and rain and sun. Some gaps were patched. Floodwaters from the nearby creek still hadn't fully receded from the stone foundation. Some planks were laid down across the gravel drive to the slanted steps.

The sun arced higher, like an archer's bow in the sky, gaining definition as it worked free of the low-hanging fog. Sweat began to trickle down my back as I balanced across the plank. My wife and children were with me, along with the dozen "young adults" from our church.

I suppose there would be an air-conditioned church in a town nearby. If anyone suggested going there, a rebellion would follow. We had lived in this community, worked here, been inside homes here, for the past week. Tomorrow we would be heading home. Besides, in the church in town somewhere, the greeters probably wouldn't embrace us as we entered.

Although I am part of another religious tradition, worshipping at inner city Pentecostal and Bible churches had been a regular part of my growing-up. Maybe that's why the two hours we spent with our brothers and sisters in Christ in this ramshackle church, bullfrogs croaking loudly from the stream that ran into the Mississippi a half mile away, left a fingerprint of God upon me. I can't detail the entire service, of course. But like an indelible stamp of personhood, God left his fingerprint on my heart that morning—"You are mine."

It can be anywhere, at any time. God places his hand upon you, lays his fingerprint upon your heart, and says that you are his. A child of God.

The Calling

Stated like that, it seems as though heaven cracks open and a sign of calling flashes in bright neon colors. Maybe it works that way for some people. For most people, however, it is comfort and affirmation in the place they already are. God has already gifted you precisely for the calling he has visited upon you. Instead of trying to find the neon signs in the heavens, we faithfully tend to the calling God has given us on this earth.

It is also true, nonetheless, that God calls us to places we don't always want to go. Sometimes we sing "I'll go where you send me," but we're mapping the highways in our minds. All Christians have a calling, no matter what their religious tradition, no matter worshippers in a dusky Delta church or in a lavish cathedral. Nonetheless, some bear a special calling.

Consider the story we have traced thus far. How far would

the Israelites have gotten without the heroic leadership of Zerubbabel and Sheshbezzar? How solid would their leadership have been without the revelation of God's law by Ezra? And how long would this worship have lasted without Nehemiah's intervention with Artaxerxes? This was not an overnight process. The stages lasted over a century. Often overlooked in the high drama of this story, however, is the role of two men—unfortunately relegated to that category of minor prophets. We are surprised, until we look carefully, at how important the roles of Haggai and Zechariah are in planting the kingdom of God in the threatened soil of Jerusalem.

I am reminded, as a lifelong fan of J. R. R. Tolkien, of the unassuming hobbit Bilbo Baggins, the center-stage character of *The Hobbit,* which is itself an introduction to *The Lord of the Rings.* The thing about Bilbo is that he would like to be anywhere but center stage. He is entirely content in his comfortable, sandy hobbit hole, and has no great aspirations to go anywhere else, or to be anyone else, all the days of his life. Yet it is this very unremarkable creature who is called to heroic deeds that change the shape of his world.

I am a great deal like Bilbo Baggins. I suspect most Christians are. What happens when we are *called out* and *called to* speak the truth boldly? The only thing I can rely on is the word of Jesus: "But make up your mind not to worry beforehand how you will defend yourselves. For I will give you words and wisdom that none of your adversaries will be able to resist or contradict" (Luke 21:14–15). I confess that even with this promise, I still feel insecure defending the Word of God; I need to supplement my study of the Bible with study of different guides, such as *Evangelism Explosion* by D. James Kennedy, to make my own words intelligible and coherent.

As the chronology at the beginning of this book points out, two other important prophets spoke of God's will during the bleak period of the Israelites' captivity. The great prophet Jeremiah spoke during the years immediately preceding the exile (approximately 626–586 BC). His message is marked by warnings, but also by a righteous anger for a people who neglect his warnings. Like a physician diagnosing spiritual illness, Jeremiah specifically names the sins of the people. They worshipped idols (and even engaged in child sacrifice); they lived for themselves. Yet, as God's prophet, Jeremiah affirms repeatedly that he speaks out of love for his people. At one point he pleads with God:

> Although our sins testify against us,
> O LORD, do something for the sake of your
>   name....
> You are among us, O LORD,
>   and we bear your name;
>   do not forsake us! (Jeremiah 14:7, 9)

This is the voice of someone interceding in spiritual anguish. If, in fact, Jeremiah is the author of Lamentations as most biblical scholars agree, the intense poetry of that book may be read as a loving plea to God for a distraught people.

Jeremiah is sometimes called the Prophet of Doom, which is not a very accurate name since his warnings are given in love. However, if Jeremiah is a Prophet of Doom, Ezekiel must be called the Prophet of Hope. Ezekiel not only lived through the time of great upheaval and captivity, but was in fact among the exiles when Nebuchadnezzar first besieged Jerusalem in 597 BC. In 586 BC, Nebuchadnezzar thoroughly destroyed the city and the temple, plundering them and setting everything ablaze. Ezekiel's prophetic mission endured in exile until 571 BC.

What was Ezekiel's message to a forsaken people? His name means "God is strong," and that name also shapes the central thrust of his prophecy. God is sovereign. In a time when all is changed, when desolation seems the *status quo*, and when the old verities seem hopelessly lost, Ezekiel prophesies a new Jerusalem and a new temple. His prophecy may be summarized in the very last verse of his book: "And the name of the city from that time on will be: THE LORD IS THERE" (48:35). Here is his message of hope: In the midst of our forsakenness, God is there.

These are the words our ears ache to hear. This is the message for which we stand on tiptoe in anticipation. In our darkest night, the Lord is there. At our time of sorrow, when nothing makes sense, the Lord is there. As in Ezekiel's vision of dry bones made alive by God's breath, in our desert places, the Lord is there. This message constituted Israel's history. It linked them with more than mere traditions or rituals, now all ruptured into fragmented memories. It linked them, rather, with the living God, sovereign in all of history. That message is no less ours to claim today. The Lord is still there—right here in our presence.

Jeremiah and Ezekiel prophesied at the beginning of the exile, the one proclaiming powerful warnings, the other pumping hope like air itself into a defeated people. Two other important prophets carried on the great task during later years of the exile. Haggai and Zechariah had the more specific task of leading the people to a deeper, firmer understanding of living in God's presence. They are sometimes called "minor prophets," a huge misnomer. At no time is the clear word of God "minor." For their time, and at their place, Haggai and Zechariah were major figures indeed.

The prophets were both called to grant clarity, but very substantial differences separated them. Haggai (meaning "festal") spoke directly to his present age. The core of his message is the twofold theme of the consequences of obedience and disobedience. Moreover, he repeatedly provides words of encouragement. On the other hand, Zechariah (meaning "the Lord remembers") was a prophet of things in the future. Yes, he calls for spiritual renewal, but he does so with an inner eye that clearly perceives the reign of the Messiah.

The historical context of the two prophets is quite easily determined. Haggai's messages can be broken down into four "sermons" preached during the second year—520 BC—of King Darius's reign. Apparently Haggai was an elderly man, in his seventies, at the time. Zechariah arrived with the group under Zerubbabel in 538 BC, but began his messages at the same time as Haggai under the freedoms provided by King Darius. Zechariah prophesied until approximately 480 BC.

THE MESSAGES

Although Haggai's messages were preached over a period of four months, in four different installments, a progressive unity guides them. One of the remarkable features of his messages is the frequent repetition of "The Lord Almighty says," or a close variation of it. Haggai immediately establishes under whose authority he speaks.

The first message (see 1:1–11) calls the people to get to work building the temple. Too many personal concerns have intruded; too few spiritual concerns have been pursued. The consequences of such a life are clear. Having expected much, the people have received little; having focused on their own desires, they have paid scant attention to God's will. Therefore, Haggai points out the reality: "Because of you the heavens have withheld their dew and the earth its crops" (v. 10).

Two interesting things occur. How might we have responded to Haggai? Maybe laugh him off as a wacko? Maybe argue—"Wait a minute. I need a roof over my head. Surely you exaggerate!" But Zerubbabel and the people acknowledge the truth of Haggai's words. In turn, in his second message Haggai encourages the people and promises peace and glory. Here is the central theme of his message: "'Be strong, all you people of the land,' declares the LORD" (2:4). Be strong. That encouragement ripples through the entire account of rebuilding the temple. We thirst for those words as we would for a pure stream. Haggai makes it clear that the stream flows for us when we commit ourselves to the will of God.

The theme of God's strength being *our* strength continues in the third and fourth messages. The focus shifts slightly, however. The third warns against relapse into sin but ends with positive encouragement: "From this day on I will bless you" (v. 19). The fourth foresees future struggles but promises that the power of the Lord will be with his people.

In his messages, then, Haggai charts a clear course for God's people. First, we recognize where our sinful will has supplanted God's will, and we change the equation. Second, we recognize that our strength lies in the Lord. Third, trying daily to walk in the way of the Lord, we receive his blessing. Fourth, in that walk we enjoy the strength of almighty God.

Zechariah also speaks to the people in their present condition and need, but his method couldn't be more different. Bolstered by analogies and allegories, laced with rhapsodic poetry that reminds one of King David, Zechariah's far-reaching vision also sees the people of God many centuries in the future and the advent of the Messiah. In a sense, to understand Haggai we have to read his words as an Israelite living in a largely ruined city. To understand Zechariah, we have to read his words right where we are—on this side of the incarnation.

The first mystical visions of Zechariah establish themes that align him squarely in the tradition of Old Testament history and prophets. Chapter 1 centers upon a promise held out numerous times to God's people: "'Return to me,' declares the LORD Almighty, 'and I will return to you'" (1:3). Chapter 2 promises protection for his people. Although the people were measuring and rebuilding walls for protection, God promises they will be protected by his immeasurable strength. "'I myself will be a wall of fire around it,' declares the LORD, 'and I will be its glory within'" (2:5). Why is this? Because, as the Lord says, "whoever touches you touches the apple of his eye" (v. 8). That phrase reaches back to Moses (see Deut. 32:10) and King David (see Ps. 17:8).

Having established continuity with the past, in chapter 3 Zechariah signals some undercurrents. They are not overt. Yet they hook our attention, as if to say—"There's something more going on here." Earlier I made reference to Tolkien's *The Hobbit*, precursor to the magnificent *Lord of the Rings* trilogy. It is very possible, as I did the first time, to read the trilogy absorbed completely by the high adventure. But then you start to reflect on things in the adventure. They keep coming to mind. Here the great "I wonder if ..." comes into play. The gift of human imagination, one of the greatest gifts God has given us, begins to work. We start to see the events in different contexts and begin to see new significance. Here in Zechariah we start to read from our side of the incarnation.

On the immediate, narrative level, the events of chapter 3 seem pretty straightforward. It describes the consecration of Jeshua as high priest (see Ezra 2:2). Jeshua, however, also stands as representative of the people before the Lord; consequently, Zechariah reveals a scene in heaven where an angel cleanses Jeshua for his role. Then Zechariah describes events that could only belong to the future.

Remember here that Jeshua and its variant Joshua were common Old Testament names. The Greek equivalent in the New Testament is Jesus. All these names mean "the Lord saves." The fascinating tie Zechariah makes lies between the present and future. Speaking to Jeshua and his fellow priests, Zechariah says that they are "symbolic of things to come" (3:8)—specifically, "I am going to bring my servant, the Branch" (v. 8). Now we're on different ground, recalling the prophetic language of 150 years earlier (see Isa. 4:2; 11:1; and the detailed messianic prophecy of Isa. 53; see also Jer. 23:5; 33:15). The transition is in place, the connections made.

In the house where I was raised, we had a small sitting room generously stuffed with an old sofa, my mother's sewing machine, and an old chipped and stained Philco upright radio. As a young boy I sat next to my dad on the sofa following the adventures of such worthies as the Green Hornet, the Shadow, and the Lone Ranger. Yes, this was in the age of television, but my folks saw no reason to invest in one. We visited the library every other Saturday; we had music; and we had the old Philco—a crackling, whizzing machine that caught about half the action and dialogue. We filled in the gaps by guesswork until one day Dad called in the neighborhood handyman who replaced all the tubes and wiring. And like that, our hearing and understanding were fixed.

In such a way, perhaps, Zechariah cleans out the Israelites' ears. We need a two-way vision: for the present and for things to come. If we lose either direction, we short-change our Christian calling. "But it's so hard," we say. "I'm working two jobs now just to get by." Or, "This world has caused me so much grief I'm just going to give up on it and ponder my treasure in heaven." Indeed, most of us do stumble around in this life, peering about as if through a glass too darkly. We try to pick ourselves up, but the knees of our jeans seem caked with mud. It's too hard to take another step, and we feel frozen in a field like a scarecrow left out in the snow.

The beauty of these passages in Zechariah lies in their full recognition of our need. He is not a prophetic dreamer. He possesses the God-given gift of two-way vision. Thus in chapter 4 he specifically addresses our human condition— our aspirations, but also our fears and frailties. First, he reminds us where our strength lies: "This is the word of the Lord to Zerubbabel: 'Not by might nor by power, but by my Spirit,' says the Lord Almighty" (v. 6). Sometimes we still want to act like two-year-olds: "I'll do it all by myself!" Grow up. Let the power of the Holy Trinity help you. But second, it also may be that we don't feel ourselves capable of doing anything for God's kingdom—an idea we discussed in an earlier chapter. Zechariah responds, "Who despises the day of small things?" (v. 10). Indeed, as we noted before, little is much when God is in it—just like the manger in Bethlehem.

Beginning in chapter 6 a series of powerful allusions to the Messiah appears.

The first of these unites the formerly separate offices of priest and king: "Here is the man whose name is the Branch, and he will branch out from his place and build the temple of the Lord. It is he who will build the temple of the Lord, and he will be clothed with majesty and will sit and rule on his throne" (vv. 12–13).

The writer of Hebrews makes clear the fulfillment: "For every house is built by someone, but God is the builder of everything…. Christ is faithful as a son over God's house. And we are his house, if we hold on to our courage and the hope of which we boast" (3:4, 6). Thus, we are the New Testament temple, ruled over by our High Priest and King, Jesus.

Second, Zechariah tells us how to live in that temple, again echoing a theme coursing through the entire Bible. Fasting, he states, can easily become a public show of piety rather than a drawing close to God (see 7:5). Instead comes the admonition: "Administer true justice; show mercy and compassion to one another. Do not oppress the widow or the fatherless, the alien or the poor" (vv. 9–10). We don't have to read far into the New Testament to realize that justice, mercy, and compassion constitute the three major social themes of Jesus' preaching. Take it a step further, though. On the cross Jesus *enacted* justice—he paid the full requirement for our sin. He *provided* mercy—we are incapable of working out this salvation by ourselves. He *showed* compassion—making this sacrifice for the pure fact that he loves us.

Third, this compassionate, just, and merciful High Priest and King is also our great Deliverer. Zechariah foresees the Messiah's triumphant return into Jerusalem on Palm Sunday:

> Rejoice greatly, O Daughter of Zion!
> Shout, Daughter of Jerusalem!
> See, your king comes to you,
> righteous and having salvation,
> gentle and riding on a donkey,
> on a colt, the foal of a donkey. (9:9)

He goes on to say that the Messiah, riding on a donkey, will replace "the war-horses from Jerusalem" (v. 10), thereby ushering in a new era of peace. Moreover, Zechariah rejoices in song over the salvation that will come on that day:

> The LORD their God will save them on that day
> as the flock of his people.
> They will sparkle in his land
> like jewels in a crown.
> How attractive and beautiful they will be!
> (vv. 16–17)

Jesus' crown was plaited from thorns (see Matt. 27:29). But that isn't the end of the matter for the Messiah. It never was, is, or shall be. In the book of Revelation, John sees one "like a son of man" (1:13)—the name by which Jesus identified himself—who says to the church of Smyrna: "Be faithful, even to the point of death, and I will give you the crown of life" (2:10). How can that be? Later in the revelation, John is shown a picture of the judge coming to harvest the earth for final judgment. Here's what he sees: "I looked, and there before me was a white cloud, and seated on the cloud was one 'like a son of man,' with a crown of gold on his head and a sharp sickle in his hand" (14:14). Then Zechariah's prophecy will be fulfilled. Those who love the Lord will be the jewels in his crown.

Other passages in Zechariah follow a similar pattern of fulfillment in the Messiah. For example, the allegory of the two shepherds in chapter 11 certainly clarifies Jesus' statement, "I am the good shepherd" (John 10:11). Similarly, the tale of the thirty pieces of silver, signifying the minimal amount paid for a slave, deeply colors and enriches the betrayal of Jesus. Most powerful, however, are the premonitory figures in chapters 12 through 14. The clarity and force of these are startling.

Chapter 12 depicts the mourning for the one we ourselves have pierced: "They will look on me, the one they have pierced, and they will mourn for him as one mourns for an only child" (v. 10). We should take careful note of the fact that the cause for this event, however, arises from a "spirit of grace and supplication" (v. 10). Thus grace and our supplication meet in the piercing of the only Son.

The day this occurs, however, will be a terrible day. Humans might see the dying of an only child on Calvary; from the eternal view (into which Zechariah is permitted a momentary glimpse) all heaven and earth are twisted in warfare where the only Son overcomes evil. In Zechariah's vision everything shifts like a Goya painting: "On that day there will be no light, no cold or frost. It will be a unique day, without daytime or nighttime—a day known to the Lord" (14:6–7). Perhaps the clearest contextual allusion here is to the crucifixion given the foregoing elements such as the piercing, the crown (of thorns), and the grace of God's only child. But it is possible also that the prophecy alludes to the second coming with its tribulation in the solar system. Whatever the case, Zechariah makes his primary point clear: "The Lord will be king over the whole earth. On that day there will be one Lord, and his name the only name" (v. 9).

Now comes the question. What do we make of it all? How do we tie the threads together?

The fact is they don't all weave neatly together. Prophecy isn't like that. Despite the best efforts of theologians and linguists, we see strands, some of them parallel, but seldom a perfect whole. Consider, for example, the prophetic vision of John in the revelation. The number of articles and books on this rather brief vision would fill a very large bookcase. Why is this?

In a sense, differing prophecies work together like the experiences in various churches I noted at the beginning of this chapter. I could have mentioned many more. For example, when we have gone on family camping trips we have always made it a point to worship at some nearby church on Sunday morning. One time we happened to camp overlooking the Pacific Ocean while I was doing research at nearby Stanford University. At the start of our morning worship in this small church, a stunning California girl—deeply tanned with shining blonde hair and dressed in a dazzling white robe edged in gold—walked to the pulpit. My youngest daughter, all of three years old at the time, leaned over and whispered to me.

"Daddy, is that an angel?"

"No, honey. That's the minister."

"Oh."

I mention these highly diverse worship experiences for one simple fact. No matter the congregation or denomination, we gather to meet the Lord. Moreover, all these experiences have been formative upon my own spiritual life. The term *Christian* extends beyond one local church and is finally defined not just as a doctrinal community but as a family of believers. Each experience has enriched my knowledge of God.

Prophecy works something like that. Certainly it is God's way of unifying the Old Testament and the New Testament churches. Didn't Jesus himself say, "Do not think that I have come to abolish the Law or the Prophets; I have not come to abolish them but to fulfill them" (Matt. 5:17)? Such a case we find with Zechariah especially. Those things he saw dimly Jesus sees clearly.

If we see prophecy as a means for unity, a second quality is applicable here. Prophecy always begins where the people are. It's grounded in gritty reality. We sometimes think of prophecy as something vaporous and apart from life. Both Haggai and Zechariah, in line with other Old Testament prophets, are intent upon calling the people here and now back to what is right in God's eyes. Like judges they declare this is what is right: "Here is where you have gone wrong. Here is what has to be done about it." As such, their voices are no less pertinent today.

The third thing we notice among the prophets, and especially here in the rebuilding of the temple, is the pattern of restoration. As we have seen throughout this study, the physical rebuilding of Jerusalem and the temple paralleled the spiritual rebuilding of the people. For that latter work, if you will, the prophets held the blueprint.

Now we can see the end of the matter, can't we? We've discovered the final direction, where the whole thing has been leading. To make a beginning is to make an ending, for on the way we are working to get somewhere, to arrive at some place. And in this journey of rebuilding the temple, and also in our own lives, there is only one possible ending, even if it might surprise us beyond belief. When we do God's will, when we realize what he has done for us, that one and only possible ending is joy. But it is a special joy, as we see in the next chapter.

CHAPTER 11

Living in Celebration

Reading: Nehemiah 8—9

I am sure that there are some mothers whose idea of heaven is simply a place where they won't have to cook anymore. Maybe they'll be waited on more often than they were on earth; maybe their celestial bodies won't need the coarse grub that passes for food here. If the lion and the lamb lie down together, after all, won't the cow be safe? Or maybe we'll all be vegetarians, ceaselessly plucking ripe, plump fruit in the new Eden. That would solve the problem.

Except for my mother. She would have wanted a wedding feast and she would have wanted to be at the very center of its preparation. One would think she would have had enough of it. As one of three daughters of a widow during the Great Depression, she contributed to the family's meager resources by working at a bakery. Welfare assistance at that time consisted of a weekly gallon of milk obtained from the fire station. Her financial status did not improve a great deal when she married my father, a young teacher with great skill at baseball and in the classroom but with a painfully small salary to raise four children. Yet they hosted book clubs and occasionally a penniless student who needed a place to stay. They fed all such guests lavishly.

My childhood memories focus often on the parties at our house—cakes and pies and assorted sweets for a room full of people. As I got older I would sneak out of bed after the party and eat my fill. And there would be meals for the relatives that would take one's breath away around that big old dining room table. Still today, I have people remind me of those happy times spent in our living room or dining room, places of great laughter and gracious food.

Certain events Mother insisted upon hosting. The annual gathering of "the cousins" somehow squeezed into my parents' tiny condominium of later years. New Year's Day, when the table would be laid out with a buffet of foods to which we helped ourselves during breaks in the Rose Bowl. But especially each of her children's—and their spouses'—birthdays. I can see that table of honor—I can nearly smell its rich scents. The Swiss steak piled in layers on the platter. A half-dozen different vegetables, including the ones I liked but nobody else did—sweet potatoes and beets. It was a celebration to make your heart pound.

Often my wife asked Mom for recipes for a favorite dish. Only a few were ever written down, and these my mother modified to suit her own creative whimsy. When Pat asked Mom for a recipe for a certain cake once, it went something like: "… a heaping cup of … a generous teaspoon of …" But it would never taste the same. Perhaps Mom's recipes went all the way back to those days when she worked in the bakery during the Depression for ten cents an hour. She took something of infinitely more worth from that time than the wage. She took a spirit of celebration, a festivity that enriched all who knew her. I don't know, of course, what kind of recipes, if any, will be cooked in heaven. But if they are, I know that heaven is a still brighter place by Mom's being there.

At the close of our earthly lives, we slip over into eternal joy. That's the true story. So too the true story of Ezra and Nehemiah is more than the struggle, the soul-twisting anxieties, and the life-threatening attacks. Of course, it is unrealistic to consider joy apart from the gritty events of life's journey. I may confidently testify to my mother's place in glory; I cannot do so without remembering the hard passage of her dying. Sometimes we hold up a false ideal of "Christian joy." We are all scrub-faced and smiling in the portrait. None of us has crooked teeth. The false ideal becomes downright deceitful when we begin to believe that there is something like an easy seven-step plan, the top rung of which has us garbed in radiant white, unspotted and above the affairs— even above the Sanballats—of this world. I call this deceitful because it goes precisely against the way Jesus walked and taught, and certainly it lies counter to every powerful reality revealed in this testimony of Ezra and Nehemiah.

Take an overview once more of those harried laborers of Nehemiah. Surrounded by enemies from the outside, they had to work under the constant threat of attack. Yes, they had posted a guard, but would it be strong enough? There were so many of the enemy; so few of them. Fear is a devastating emotion. It eats at the core of a person, diminishing one's personhood like melting ice.

Then there was the work itself. Bad enough to have to labor hard under the Judean sun, carrying and hoisting rocks and mortar—but to have to do so with a sword at one's side! And when they were ready to collapse at night, stinking of sweat, they shivered under makeshift coverings because the houses were still not rebuilt. They were prodded awake the next morning to one more day of filthy, hard labor. It enervated them physically. Exhaustion crept along the wall with each new rock put in place.

Worst of all, perhaps, was the fact that many of the workers were separated from their families who were left behind on outlying homesteads. Not only had they forfeited their duties on their own farms, but also the separation seemed to widen day by day into a desperate longing. One can be in a crowd of thousands and still feel like the loneliest person alive. Stripped of those you love and all those routines that mark life with the solace of familiarity, loneliness can rise up like a beast.

This is the reality. Let's not have any platitudes about the joyful life here. Nor about our own. Sometimes our joy is forged out of a crucible of suffering. Where does it come from then? Are we doomed to wander the face of this earth like hopeless pilgrims, weighed down by the sack of our own tribulation? Is there no hope? Indeed, such a view would be as false to Scripture as would the view that the Christian's life should be nonstop bliss. Often the Psalms are referred to as the Songs of Hope. For example, Psalm 43:5 recognizes the reality and the hope:

> Why are you downcast, O my soul?
>   Why so disturbed within me?
> Put your hope in God, for I will yet praise him,
>   my Savior and my God.

The pattern isn't limited to the Psalms, where it beats like a steady rhythm behind nearly every song. It threads throughout other Old Testament passages. Surely one of the most consoling passages is Isaiah 40:31:

> Those who hope in the LORD will renew their
>   strength.
> They will soar on wings like eagles; they will run

and not grow weary, they will walk and not be
faint.

The progression in that familiar verse is interesting.
Some of us will soar like eagles. Some run as if we could go
on forever. But I suspect that many of us wish only to
walk—to keep up the daily pace of life—without fainting
under the pressure. That is celebration—the enactment of a
joyful hope in the very center of our life's challenges. Such
was very much the case with Nehemiah and his people.

THE FESTIVAL OF CELEBRATION

The Israelites didn't just step overnight into celebration. Even
as the last rows of the wall were being set, a nervous tension
crept through the air. For one thing, Sanballat still had tricks
up his sleeve. One such was to invite Nehemiah to one of the
outlying villages to talk truce. Now that would be a relief. All
the worry would evaporate. But Nehemiah smelled the rat
inside Sanballat's clothes. Nehemiah rejected the offer, making it clear that it was his task to work on the wall.

Sanballat had another ruse. The fifth time he extended
the invitation he left the letter unsealed so it could be read
and its message spread like a rumor. This letter differed sub-
stantially. It rumored sedition against King Artaxerxes. It
suggested that Nehemiah wanted to establish himself as sole
king in Judah. But Nehemiah had prepared for this too. Not
only did he denounce it as a lie, he likely sent a messenger
back to Artaxerxes to allay any concerns the king may have
had when the rumor reached him.

Still Sanballat wasn't done. He manufactured a threat on
Nehemiah's life designed to sap the morale of the workers. A
man called Shemiah told Nehemiah that men were coming

to kill him, and that he had better hide out in the temple and lock the doors. But again, Nehemiah saw through the plot and in the name of the Lord refused to go (see 6:11–12). In fact, these very schemes turned on the enemies "because they realized that this work had been done with the help of our God" (6:16). Their self-confidence, rather than that of the Israelites, was destroyed.

The work went apace. The walls were finished; the gates were set in place. It must have been an astounding sight for those laborers who had worked so hard. For the first time they could step back and look at the whole. They could wander about, enjoy the spaciousness of the city with its beautiful new temple. There was only one problem. At this point there were few houses, few shops, and few people. This posed two dangers. First, there was a spiritual danger. Jerusalem was to be God's community, the cornerstone of his kingdom of peace on earth. Second, it posed a tactical danger. With an area this large, an enemy could easily attack remote areas of the wall and be inside the city in minutes. Therefore, Nehemiah engages the last step toward celebration. He brings the people together.

CELEBRATION IN COMMUNITY

Ever the careful strategist, Nehemiah had taken practical steps against the immediate tactical danger. For example, instead of opening the gates at sunrise, as would be customary, he imposes an order that they would not be opened "until the sun is hot." The point of the tactical countermove is clear. It preempts an early surprise attack and gives the guards the benefit of a clear study of who is waiting to enter. Moreover, Nehemiah makes arrangements for each house to post a guard in addition to the guard units around the city. The problem is that there were still so very few houses.

The lack of houses in Jerusalem signified more than an underpopulated city. Like shards of pottery flung over vast spaces, the rubble of housing represented a breakdown in the Jewish community. Compare this community, for example, with the people under Moses. Isolated, wandering, bewildered in the desert, they nonetheless had the sense of being God's chosen people. Thus their great confession of communal faith: "Hear, O Israel: The LORD our God, the LORD is one. Love the LORD your God with all your heart and with all your soul and with all your strength" (Deut. 6:4–5). This confession, known yet today as the great Shema (literally "hear"), had seldom been heard in the time of Nehemiah. The people had been two hundred years in stages of exile and were not permitted to live as a small "nation within a nation." They were driven apart. Genealogical records, so essential to Jewish life, had fallen into tatters. Even as Nehemiah tried to make sense of the records of those who had first returned from exile, new problems arose, for these families and clans had settled wherever they could about the countryside. What could weld them together? What did they hold in common to become a community responding to "Hear, O Israel: The LORD our God, the LORD is one"? That common bond lay in the rediscovery of God's law.

THE BASIS FOR CELEBRATION

We tend to think of laws in terms of restrictions. Especially in the United States, perhaps, where the Constitution was written to protect individual freedoms, we become suspicious of any enactments that may limit those freedoms. The very freedom that we have heightens our suspicion of any imposition upon it. In such a climate of thought, which sees additional laws as something like a dark cloud on a distant horizon that threatens the sunny brightness of individual freedom, we find it hard to conceive of law itself as a good and positive thing. Yet we have to admit, as we have explored earlier, that the constitutional basis for our law is also at once the basis for our freedom—that without law we would have mere anarchy, and that in the absence of law we would have a kind of social reversion to principles where only the strong survive, feeding off the weaker members of society. Even granting that, however, it is possible to see a system of law not just as a protector of freedom, not just as an agenda for social order, but also, shockingly, as a living relationship of loving community. That is precisely the state between God's laws and us. Rather than just restrictive rules of what we should not do, God's law is liberating and designed to build a loving relationship. In fact, the central passage of Nehemiah, where Ezra reads the law of God to God's people, pretty much abolishes the common image of a baleful, vengeance-seeking Lord.

We have to remind ourselves, however, that in this story of Nehemiah we are looking at events from the far side of the incarnation. Our greatest evidence of God's love today is his son, Jesus, for here a God so great that he made the world now made himself so small he could redeem the very creation he loves. On that other side of the incarnation, the people had different sorts of revelation. They had accounts of God's gracious acts to his chosen people, for example. They had the prophets speaking in God's name. But most important, always, they had the Book of the Law—the Pentateuch, the first five books of the Bible. Therein lay God's will for them, his promises to them, and the framework of a love relationship.

Anticipation was high. People flowed into Jerusalem from outlying villages. They had gathered before dawn, standing nearly shoulder to shoulder in the large open square by the Water Gate. Ezra waited with them. Then, as the orange cusp of the sun shouldered over the horizon, the people called out for Ezra and the law of the Lord. Followed by thirteen chief priests, Ezra carried the Book of the Law before him and ascended a platform rising high above the people. As the sun rose, he began reading. For six straight hours he read, but for these people it was no drudgery. They lifted their hands and shouted, "Amen! Amen!" Then, in awesome respect for the Lawgiver, they bowed to the ground and worshipped God. One little catch appears: "Then they bowed down and worshiped the Lord *with their faces to the ground*" (Neh. 8:6, emphasis mine). This is the Jewish prostration, the attitude of mourning. If they bowed in respect to the awesome God, they fell to the ground in acknowledgment of how far they had fallen short of his laws.

But Nehemiah and Ezra saw the larger picture: This law is for your protection. Don't grieve. Celebrate the fact that you have a God who loves you and gives you these laws to keep you safe. They encourage the people to prepare a feast of celebration for "this day is sacred to our Lord. Do not grieve, for the joy of the Lord is your strength" (v. 10). Thereby the Festival of Booths is instituted. The people constructed makeshift shelters (booths) while they continued the celebration during the seven days that the law was read.

The Israelites learned once again that the law of the Lord was their delight. As the author of Psalm 119, a psalm praising God's law, put it: "The earth is filled with your love, O Lord; teach me your decrees" (v. 64). God's law is a revelation of his love, a means for maintaining a close walk with him on this earth.

SORROW AND CELEBRATION

An unexpected turn occurs here in the community. Having discovered the law, having been lifted from their prostration, having been delivered into celebration, those same Israelites, we would expect, would pick up their normal lives apace. Not so. They have more to learn about the nature of God. Their means for doing so, while very common to the Old Testament, has virtually died out in modern Christendom. We recognize the need to confess our sins individually, as we discussed earlier. We seldom practice that deeper recognition of ourselves known as the lament. This practice, which occurs here in Nehemiah, is a means of finding our true selves before a merciful God. It is a means of working *through* a situation *to* a better understanding of our relationship with God.

In Scripture we find two kinds of lament—individual and corporate. Perhaps many of us have felt the need for individual lament. Our contemporary culture, however, admonishes us against such emotional displays, and encourages us instead to the stiff upper lip and steely gaze: "Swallow your emotions." They are simply embarrassing to modern culture, unless, of course, they turn up on tabloid television where the camera zooms in like a microscope on the trickling tear. Our modern Christian culture has also discouraged displays of emotion. Particularly harmful to this necessary human expression are the so-called gospels of success. Purveyed by spiritual hucksters, these gospels declare that feeling good and acquiring wealth are signs of spiritual maturity and health. Setting aside the fact that nearly all the heroes of Scripture, including Jesus who resisted this very temptation, would not qualify for this fraudulent Christian church, the proclamation is destructive in its denial of human emotion.

Two trends in this peculiar gospel of success appear

today. First, such people proclaim a message that whatever we ask for, God will supply. God is just waiting to open the storehouses of heaven and pour out good jobs, new cars, salary increases, even a blemish-free complexion: "Toss your Revlon; we have God's grace." Thereby such people execute a malign perversion of God's enduring promise of *spiritual* blessings—to comfort, to guide, to heal, and to direct. While there is no question that God is ultimately responsible for our material blessings, and while we are obligated to thank and praise him for them, any religion that sees God as a cosmic Santa Claus—"pop in a prayer and pick out a blessing"—is a world away from biblical Christianity. I mention this fact in the context of the lament precisely because God may not be calling us to lives of materialistic ease, but God does call us to a servanthood that may mean sacrificial living.

One side of this fraudulent trend, then, is the expectation that God rewards our entreaties for material wealth. The other side is the equally misguided belief that Christians have no right being sad or lamenting in the first place. Indeed, in some churches your very Christianity is suspect if you don't clap your hands and wear a thousand-watt smile. "Ours is a joyful Christianity," the proclamation goes, "and we share the joy in our good cheer. If you feel downhearted, something is amiss with your faith."

Of course we have joy as a redeemed people of God. But we are also walking in a world where Jesus walked and in which we experience brokenness. Heaven alone is promised as the place where every tear shall be wiped away. If nothing else—and it is a whole lot more—the Bible is a book of knife-sharp realism, cutting through a lot of wacky ideas about grinning Christianity. It would not promise a place of no tears if it were not keenly aware of our present tears. In one of her most famous opening lines, American poet Emily Dickinson admits, "The soul has bandaged moments." And we might add, some wounds too severe for bandages to hide.

Biblically based Christianity is keenly aware of our fallenness, our suffering, and our pain. It is aware of the fact that the wicked prosper in their gospel of material wealth, but our treasure lies in heaven. It is aware of the fact that while the world laughs, often in scorn of us, we have a place waiting where there will be no tears, anguish, despair, or grief. But not here. Not now.

We experience sorrow and failure. What do we do with it? Is it spiritually legitimate to bring that sense of forsakenness and sorrow to God?

Instances of corporate lament, such as we read of in Nehemiah 9 where God's people gather collectively, are scattered throughout the Old Testament. The best-known example, surely, is Jeremiah's lament before God for the desolation of Israel. This strangely poetic book of Lamentations has been disregarded to a large extent, yet it bears a telling power and lesson. Jeremiah begins the lament with a description of the desolation of Israel as a bleak and cheerless land (see 1:1–11). Then he reveals the burden on his heart. He acknowledges the cause for that condition as Israel's waywardness (see vv. 12–22). Throughout this first chapter, however, the lament is also intensely personal. Jeremiah weeps for the people (see v. 16). His heart is in distress, and he laments his inner tumult before God (see v. 20).

What surprises us about Jeremiah's lament, and what is so often lost as we modern-day believers ponder his grief-laden words, is that his lament turns to affirmation. Darkness finds balance with light; despair with devotion; grief with rejoicing. This truly is the aim and end of a lament. One divests oneself of a suffering spirit not just as anger, nor as blame, but as catharsis. Having shed sorrow like a coat, one hopes to find a living flesh of affirmation.

With that pattern in mind, the third chapter of Jeremiah's lament may be one of the most remarkably *human* passages in Scripture. In fact, the early part of the chapter may be construed as a test case for clinical depression. It dips us so deeply into the anguish of suffering, no one can escape unmoved or unnerved. It does so, however, as if lowering us into a crucible where anguish is purified into joy.

Jeremiah feels that he walks alone through a profound darkness. He walks the waste places of his soul. His isolation is thorough and profound; it afflicts both his body and spirit. He feels walled off from human and divine contact, as if God has withdrawn to some infinitely remote place. In his relationships with humans, Jeremiah feels thoroughly degraded, utterly lacking in self-esteem, a veritable "laughingstock" like someone on display. Yet at the moment of most profound despair, he testifies, "Because of the LORD's great love we are not consumed, for his compassions never fail. They are new every morning; great is your faithfulness" (Lam. 3:22–23).

WHAT THE LAMENT DOES

The power, beauty, and importance of Jeremiah's lament and that of the Israelites with Ezra lie in several areas. First, it legitimates human emotions and the driving need to express them. Emotional release is not unseemly or inappropriate, as the modern world so often declares, but it forms an essential part of our spiritual as well as psychological makeup. The lament, furthermore, acknowledges that the God who has created us knows the creation he has made. God accepts this emotional turmoil in human nature. Moreover, he responds to it. The lament, then, is not solely an expression of despair;

it is also an expression of trust in a deeply personal relationship with the creator God. How many of us can find a place to go to lay out our deepest need and our intolerable pain? God hears us, and loves us for it.

Seen in this light, one might well describe Jesus' prayer in Gethsemane to his Father as a lament. Jesus lamented because his soul was "overwhelmed with sorrow to the point of death" (Matt. 26:38). He pleaded with God, twice, to remove the cup of suffering from him (see. vv. 39, 42). Yet he found his solace and strength, as did Jeremiah, in God's will and faithfulness, even though in his case it meant death.

That search for comfort and peace is precisely the reason for lament. We wrestle with God, not just to be lamed in the hip by his power, but to arrive at peace itself. R. C. Sproul put his finger on the dynamics in *The Holiness of God.* "God is holy. He is high above us, transcendent. In our wrestling match the goal is not final war but final peace" (201). The lament does not try to drag God down to our level; rather, it is a way of profoundly exposing our level of need to his healing action.

With such an understanding, and with certain scriptural passages for guidance, we may locate several elements of the lament. First, the lament is directed to God. Rather than simply an empty outpouring, the process of the lament assumes an active listener. James tells us to "Come near to God and he will come near to you" (4:8). The spiritual dynamics of the lament arise from the fact that one does not cry out in a void, but that one speaks with a God who listens. This is a mystery beyond our understanding; it is also the foundation of Christian belief: God hears us.

A second quality of the lament is that it is a deeply personal disclosure of the individual. Herein the lament differs from our more ordinary prayers with their patterns of praise and adoration, supplication and thanksgiving, intercession and affirmation. The lament is a personal disclosure that provides confession and expression of need. Like no other prayer, it is *about* the person praying the prayer.

Confession is, of course, an important element in all prayers. So too biblical lamenters come to God seeking to be renewed, and understanding that there can be no renewal apart from confession. Sin impedes communion with God; confession restores it. James 4, which urges us to draw near to God, tells us, furthermore, to "wash your hands, you sinners, and purify your hearts, you double-minded" (v. 8). Thereby, having confessed sin, the lamenter is also freed to express questions, fears, and needs. James continues in verse 9, "Grieve, mourn and wail." The mourning is the naked exposure of spiritual pain, but it follows upon confession. Thereby, we also return full circle to the opening chapters of our study. The lament over the sins of Israel recorded in the Chronicles involves the necessary recognition of who we are and what we need.

The final stage of the lament is affirmation. We believe God has heard our most intimate plea; we also acknowledge that as sovereign Lord he has the power to do something about our need. The final stage of the lament, then, moves from intimacy to elevation as it seeks restoration. One exalts the God who has become intimate with us, and one is restored by acknowledging the absolute authority of his will. Thereby, the purpose of the lament is not simply to expose a tattered life, but the knitting together of the loose ends of our lives in the supremacy of God's will and our loving subservience to that will. The testimony of Scripture is, "Humble yourselves before the Lord, and he will lift you up" (v. 10). The authority for that testimony comes from Jesus, who humbled himself and allowed himself to be lifted up on the cross (see Phil. 2:8). Not until we humble ourselves does God lift us up; in the very bending and brokenness, however, the act of lifting up occurs.

The same pattern applied to the Israelites coming together in their corporate lament—to recognize their sins, to sympathize with others, to restore their hearts. That they recognized their sins is manifestly clear, for after their prior feasting, they now "gathered together, fasting and wearing sackcloth and having dust on their heads" (Neh. 9:1). Each one of those actions held special significance for the Israelites. Fasting was an act of preparation and denying oneself in order to draw closer to God. Wearing sackcloth, usually a dusty gray garment, represented a dying to an old way of life and a mourning for sins committed in that old way of life. It was the visible symbol for intense inward humility. The act of sprinkling dust on one's head represented burial to the past but also a need to be resurrected to new life.

In this way the Israelites gathered. It was an unusual service, a back and forth pattern first in lamenting their own sins and those of their ancestors and then in reading from the Book of the Law. It culminated in a prayer of exultation and praise to God. No one asked, "Did God hear us?" Indeed their great God did hear, and a beautiful prayer flowed out like a fresh spring from the dust of their lamentation.

THE PRAYER OF BLESSINGS

The prayer of blessings that follows the lament occurs in several clear stages.

THE BLESSING OF GOD'S AWESOME POWER

This prayer in chapter 9 weaves together past and present in order to prepare for the future God holds. Thus it begins by beseeching God the Creator, the Giver of all life. Verses 7 through 15 deal with the relationship between God and humanity up to Sinai. The emphasis in this portion lies in verse 8: "You have kept your promise because you are righteous." Here too lies the emphasis for these Israelites gathered inside the rebuilt walls: God keeps his promises. Furthermore, this God has all power and authority to do so. Verse 10 of the prayer takes note of the fact that God in Sinai was a God of miraculous signs and wonders. Most precious among these was the giving of the Law (see v. 14). God is the worker of miracles and also the Lawgiver as they stand gathered together now.

THE BLESSING OF GOD'S COMPASSION

Verses 16 through 25 of the corporate prayer testify to God's goodness even during the Israelites' rebellious years of wandering in Sinai. Those familiar words appear—stiff-necked, arrogant, and the like—but the central message (and one can almost picture the gathered Israelites nodding tearfully here) is this: "But you are a forgiving God, gracious and compassionate, slow to anger and abounding in love" (v. 17). This is why the prayer brings up past wrongs—to remind us how great God's love and forgiveness are. And in his compassion, God stayed with his people, sending his "good Spirit to instruct them" (v. 20).

THE BLESSING OF GOD'S DELIVERANCE

The Israelites vacillated between sin and sanctity, between damnation and the divine. We catch just a glimpse of them on their knees, pledging fidelity to God; then, if we turn our heads for a split second, there they are getting into trouble again. Their spiritual wavering pained God just as much as our own does. And just as much they—and we—need a means of deliverance and restoration.

Verses 26 through 31 of the prayer chart this course of deliverance. The passage underscores once again God's great compassion (see v. 28), but remembers that time after time the Israelites' arrogance led them astray. More important, that arrogance led them away from observing God's law, the vital link in a loving relationship with God (see v. 29). They again felt this keenly with their recent rediscovery and reading of the Law. They felt the vacancy of that broken link. Nonetheless, the prayer emphasizes God's deliverance: "In your great mercy you did not put an end to them or abandon them, for you are a gracious and merciful God" (v. 31). God reached down and forged the link anew.

THE BLESSING OF GOD'S PRESENCE

The conclusion of the priestly prayer, verses 32 through 37, underscores the reason for their present rejoicing and the lifting of their lament. This God, so mighty in his deeds and majesty, is an "awesome God, who keeps his covenant of love" (v. 32). No matter who we are, no matter what we have done, we can always return to this bedrock of our faith; God keeps his covenant of love. Even when we break our side of the covenant, as the Israelites had, God keeps his (though not without consequences for the covenant-breakers, as the Israelites had experienced in their exile). For the Israelites, and for us, our lament does not crash upon shores of immovable rock, nor do we have to grind those rocks down forever. Right here, right now, whether we kneel in prayer or lie in sackcloth and ashes, God is present in his covenant of love. What a powerful affirmation that must have been to these beleaguered Israelites. So, too, to us. God, our great, awesome, compassionate, and delivering Lord, loves us as we are.

THE BLESSING OF PRAISE

In the face of such love, emotions seem to overflow. Weep or dance, sing or chant; let your heart rejoice. And

Nehemiah, who now seems to preside over the action, recognizes the need to respond to God's grace. We have to assume certain responsibilities and keep certain promises in order to reorder our lives in keeping with God's grace. Thus, in chapters 10 and 11 of Nehemiah, a series of reforms and pledges are instituted. These order one's belief. The lesson should not be lost on us. Our own response to God's grace cannot be a momentary emotional high or simply reveling in a state of renewal. Our vertical, covenantal relationship with God absolutely must extend horizontally to the community of our fellow humans, in the church and without. We bear this same responsibility as the Israelites to reform and to make that reformation known in the world.

As further testimony that we can't hide our personal renewal in some private shelter, we have the culminating Great Dance of Rejoicing on the city walls. The people could have danced inside the city, holding a private spiritual party for themselves. They could have stayed in the temple square. After all, enemies still lurked outside the gate. But in a loud and joyful procession, led by singers, priests, and musicians, they paraded atop the walls. Two great lines of marching, one clockwise and one counterclockwise, paraded up there, and they raised such a holy racket that "the sound of rejoicing in Jerusalem could be heard far away" (12:43). No, it didn't matter if Sanballat and his scurvy henchmen heard. The Lord had given the victory. That's why they marched on high.

Stop there. God has also given us the victory. His own Son entered the broken gates and visited the ruined places in our lives. He allowed himself to be lifted up on high. There was no rejoicing on that bleak knob of Golgotha. None whatsoever. But that wasn't the end of his being lifted up. That ignominious specter gave way to the crashing glory of the resurrection. And that opened the way for us into eternal rejoicing.

CHAPTER 12

Testament to Joy

Reading: Nehemiah 12:27–47

I am here to support my brother. It is not a place where I would normally choose to be. In fact, I can't remember ever having been in a courtroom, certainly not at a murder trial.

My brother sits in the same spot daily, at the end of the bench, as he has done each day for several weeks, from 9 a.m. to 5 p.m., taking notes on a nine-by-six-inch pad. I know that he has boxes of notes at home. For five years he has been scribbling them, trying to make connections like steel balls skidding across a neon-red pinball surface. If enough click in the right sequence, maybe he will find his answer to the eternal *why*.

The courtroom itself is an innocuous enough affair—fourth floor of the federal building, entered through metal detectors, zipped by a sterile elevator whose only sound is a detached, computerized feminine voice announcing the floor stops: "You have arrived at the fourth floor." "Thank you, Doris," I want to say. So far I haven't. I give the computer voice chip a different name every day. Through a pair of heavy wooden doors, the room at first looks far larger than it is. The illusion is created by spacings.

There is a large space between the bench, the witness stand, the jury box, and the rest of us. Another large space on the left for displays and evidence. The courtroom divides along the aisle. On the left, relatives of the accused. On the right, press reporters, sketch artists, and those of us who have waited five years for justice.

The defendant is led in shackles, his clothing askew. He is demonstrably a violent man, having assaulted his own lawyer in the courtroom. He turns as he shuffles, fixes my brother with a stare, then me. I find no emotion in his dark eyes. He nods to his mother, sits at the desk with a burly marshal on each side, yawns, and rests his forehead on the desk.

My brother is remembering his daughter and granddaughter. I am remembering my niece, her blonde hair and blue eyes, her wide and eager smile, and her one-year-old daughter, a portrait of her mother.

The details are not pretty. We all knew them. We just had to wait for justice to take its agonizingly slow course.

My nineteen-year-old niece was about to testify in court against this man who had raped her a year before. Shortly before the rape trial, for some inexplicable reason, the rapist was released from jail where he was serving time on another charge. And shortly before that trial, my niece and her one-year-old daughter were abducted. Several months later my niece's body was found in a nearby lake, bound and gagged with duct tape, weighted down by cement blocks chained to her body. The baby has never been found. But the bodies of others have been. A witness to the rape was found murdered. A homeless man whose identity (Social Security number) the killer stole disappeared. Another man disappeared and is presumed dead. The FBI apprehended the suspected killer in New York for using the SS number at a post office. In one way we were relieved at the capture.

Strangely, in another way, we were not at all. How does one begin to understand that sense of loss that keeps eating at the heart?

Surely not as celebration.

At my niece's funeral, the pastor opened his message to the congregation by declaring, loudly and firmly, "I'm going fishing today." So he did. He knew his audience. Teenagers bedecked in more rings and bracelets than a chain gang, sporting imaginative hairdos and decorative tattoos peeping out of surprising places, filled the front rows. All were friends of my niece. They straightened up with the first sonorous roll of the preacher's deep voice, "I'm going fishing today."

Not only did he hook our attention, he dove deep into our souls where grief dwells. But he didn't leave us there. "What others meant for evil," he declared, "God will make into good." I know that many of those teenagers were powerfully touched that day. But there is a story behind the newspaper headlines of the event that is even more important.

For the previous several months, my niece had corresponded at length with my wife. Their letters soon turned to spiritual matters until, one day, my niece made it abundantly clear that she had given her life wholly to the Lord. In fact, on her casket was displayed that handwritten letter testifying to her great and newfound love for Jesus, along with the Bible my wife had given her.

Sorrow and celebration so often collide in this life, one licking at the heels of the other.

The events of that summer of death may have caused our sense of desolation, but we are hardly alone in that despondency. The causes differ, but that state of the soul is the same. I think of the parents who find their teenage daughter's bed empty in the small hours of the morning and wait for her return. For some the waiting never ends. I think of the family gathered around the hospital bed, looking at the accident-mutilated shape of someone they love and wondering when to remove the maze of technical devices.

Sometimes celebration seems as distant as Orion. There are no city walls to dance on, and we couldn't care less about building temples.

I sometimes wonder, though, if even at those moments when celebration seems like dust in the wind that there can't be something very close to it. It is something deeper yet than celebration, like the galaxies behind Orion, like mountains behind the dust.

I wonder if that previous, more elemental thing might be joy.

Celebration is built upon, or emerges from, joy. It is not joy itself. Joy is that deeper state of quietude and certitude even when Orion collapses and the mountains fall into the sea. It is a knowing beyond knowledge of what is true, what is valuable, what is lovely. Above all perhaps, it is a glimpse of God.

Celebration places us in relation to God. We the human creatures lift our praise to the Creator. We thank God for the good things and for his faithfulness to us. Praise and thanksgiving arise from gladness of heart. We celebrate because we can't sit still! Emotions start tickling every inch of our bodies, and we've got to get up and march along the wall, dancing and singing as we go. But when one wearies of dancing there is still joy.

Joy is the deeper, more profound thing that cements the broken places in the walls of our lives. Joy moves in inexpressible passion, too profound for words, a soul-deep longing for the heart of God. It flickers brightly at different points in our lives when we might say to ourselves: "Here is the thing I have longed for all my life. Here is the person with whom I have a soul love. Here is the peace that passes understanding." But even these precious moments are but shadows of the joy in God. That is more like the adamantine testimony of faith in Hebrews 11:1 (RSV): "Now faith is the assurance of things hoped for, the conviction of things not seen."

Maybe joy is also something like this.

We take our family vacations early in the summer, before the tourists swarm like insects and the sky dulls under a gray film of exhaust. We do it when we know that during nights in the tent here in the Rocky Mountains the temperature will slip into the twenties, that in the blue morning we will push back coats we have thrown over our heads and our first breaths will be like little frosty clouds. There will be elk by the stream then; the bighorn sheep that go far into hiding in the mountains by late June will be grazing in the meadow just past the surrounding pines.

A few other campers are scattered about the campground in their pop-ups and tents. Already we can smell someone brewing coffee. Soon campfire smoke will drift like a lazy perfume in the valley. We came into Denver on Interstate 70. We clocked the distance from our first glimpse of the mountain peaks—fifty-two miles, the farthest yet. The sky was big with sunlight over the plains. It seemed we could see forever. Through Denver, I-70 loops upward, its four lanes laid down like some giant thumb squashed them into place, into the valleys, across steepening ridges. Our eyes are keen to find our turnoff. It's just a little rent in the granite, a couple of old buildings scattered about a stream that bursts out of the mountain pass in early June.

This is what we have come here for, moving up into the cobalt sky. Back on the plains of Nebraska the summer heat had already settled in. As we grilled dinner at a still nearly empty campground near Ogallala, we watched the sunset redden before an advancing storm cloud, black and thick as a swamp. We saw it miles away, crawling up into the sky, eating the sun, brushing the prairie with lightning. Out of the absolute, windless silence the distant rumble of thunder seemed alien.

But now we are through the gap and moving upward toward the bright sky, following the river's course. Granite arms close around us, drawing us up and in. At one turnoff we stop to catch the wind's breath in our faces. Far in the distance we think we see the peak we call Horseapple Mountain. At the end of the long trail, we will climb to its top and stand upon three miraculously rounded boulders, an upper one resting upon the lower two. They are huge, somehow caught in a rock-hard catcher's glove that has held them for eons. I have a picture of my son standing atop them. "King of the Horseapples," I tell him.

But that is still miles ahead. We only think it is the mountain we see.

The road switchbacks upward. No one drives fast. There is no reason to. We have come here to go slowly, not just to get someplace. My wife comments on the panorama, giving me a video report I can only fill in by quick glances. The road seems dangled in space. We crawl up past the stands of pine, great floes of snow still glistening pearl-like among their reddish trunks. And everywhere, everywhere the run-off water flows.

It flows sheeted across the roadbed or it thickens through tunnels, erupting out of the cliff side of the road. Still we crawl upward.

Then down. The van rides in second gear, like a team of oxen held in rein. One foot taps the brake now and then. And the long, lush valley opens before us. The water cascades all around. At the turnoffs there are signs posted: "Do Not Drink the Water." I want to drink the water. I want its icy cold on my tongue, over my face.

But the sign warns us away. "The water," it says, "carries the parasite giardia. Don't drink."

We pull off by a mountain lake where there are no other cars. "I'll only be a minute," I apologize to my wife. But she knows what I am doing, what I am about to do. "I'll never be truly content," I tell her, "until I drink from that stream." It is more than a stream; it is a cascade, a torrent through the ice down to the lake. My son climbs out of the van with me. Truly he is too much like his father.

The water cascades like bolts of blue sky and white cloud all mixed madly together. Together Joel and I climb among the white rocks while Pat watches. We find a place where we can kneel down at the water's edge, cup it in one palm and drink. It is every bit as fiercely cold as I expected. We splash each other in laughter and carry water in cupped and leaking palms back to where Pat sits, watching the stream wash all the cold away.

I want so much to keep drinking.

We turn back to the van now, to the common joy of our camping. I wonder briefly if I'll get sick, then remember the bite of cold water under the sunswept sky. I will never forget that moment.

If we measure our joy by increments of happiness in this life, it seems to me that it will always be at risk. Illness does come; Sanballats do inflict their perverse designs; disappointment and heartache may seem our closest friends. Monstrous murderers violate every shred of human decency. Even when our walls lie in ruins, however, we still kneel before the fresh, clear flow of Jesus' grace. He alone can carry us in joy when all the walls seem ruined.

Flow, river. Flow.

READERS' GUIDE

*for Personal Reflection or
Group Discussion*

ॐ

Readers' Guide

છ્ઝ

INTRODUCTION

1. What vision does the Lord give Ezekiel?

2. How does this vision pertain to Israel's situation?

3. What did God promise to do for Israel?

4. How do God's promises to Israel fit into our own circumstances today?

CHAPTER 1: LIVING IN EXILE

1. What two promises does God give to Abram?

2. What does the root word for *exile* mean?

3. What does the author compare exile to in his own experience?

4. What does the author mention as the root cause of exile in our own time?

5. The author calls fear "liberating." What does he mean by this?

6. According to the author, why do we cling to our state of exile?

7. What are the first two steps out of exile?

CHAPTER 2: FORGIVENESS IN FETTERS

1. What, primarily, does forgiveness involve?

2. What are three modern impediments that keep us from showing God the full extent of our need?

3. What's wrong with the idea that we're "pretty good people"?

4. What is "the victim mentality"? How does it prevent us from seeking God's forgiveness?

5. What does the author mean by "generic grace"? How does it differ from "spiritual grace"?

6. How does a proper understanding of the person of Jesus affect our understanding of grace?

CHAPTER 3: THE CAPTIVE NATION

1. What must we do to understand the true nature of our need and the answers for our need?

2. What are the two parts of a Russian proverb that Aleksandr Solzhenitsyn references in his great novel, *The Gulag Archipelago*?

3. What is the first step in spiritual dying?

4. How do we begin to remedy our condition of spiritual dying?

5. Whom did God raise up to release Israel from bondage? Was this individual a believer in God or not? What does this say about how God works in history?

6. What two obscure figures did God raise up to begin Israel's restoration?

7. What did the first Israelite exiles see when they first glimpsed home?

CHAPTER 4: AT GOD'S ALTAR

1. What does the Hebrew word translated *altar* literally mean? How do sacrifices presented to God by humans achieve atonement or reconciliation?

2. Can you give a definition of priesthood? Who are priests, and what is their function?

3. What four things did the altar represent for the Israelites?

4. Through whom did the Israelite priesthood begin?

5. Do Christian churches have altars? If so, what are they for?

6. What was the very first thing the Israelites did upon returning from exile?

7. What are three fears holding today's Christians in a powerful grip? How does each one of these inhibit a proper relationship to God?

CHAPTER 5: BUILDING SPIRITUAL FOUNDATIONS

1. What is the first step in rebuilding a broken spiritual life? What does it entail?

2. What does God say to us when we ask him to come to the altar of our hearts?

3. How does true Christianity differ from the existential religions so prominent today?

4. Christianity is solely a relationship between the believer and God: true or false? Support your answer from the author's observations in this chapter.

5. What did the Israelites do next after rebuilding the altar of the Lord? What did they do in the middle of this activity?

6. What are some of the reasons Rick Warren gives for belonging to a church and regularly attending its services? Is there such a thing as being a Christian apart from a church community? Why or why not?

CHAPTER 6: PEOPLE OF AUTHENTIC FAITH

1. The author identifies authentic faith as a longing of every Christian. Do you think this is true? Has it always been true for you? For other Christians you know?

2. What did the people do after they completed the rebuilding of the temple in 516 BC, exactly seventy years after its destruction? What must fill the temple besides the joy of praise?

3. What was going on in the Persian Empire between the years of the completion of the temple (516 BC) and the coming of Ezra (458 BC)? What does this tell us about how God works in history on behalf of his people?

4. When Ezra arrived, what three things did he bring with him?

5. What three things were contained in Artaxerxes' commission? How does the third point relate to our situation today?

6. What are the three gauges of authentic faith?

7. Why does God give us his divine law?

8. What three important truths that God revealed to Ezra ground our faith?

CHAPTER 7: PEOPLE OF FIDELITY

1. What is the final step the Israelites must take for the rebuilding process to be completed?

2. When Nehemiah heard about the plight of the returned exiles, what was the first thing he did?

3. What is the difference between authentic faith and fidelity?

4. There are three parts to Nehemiah's prayer. What are they?

5. What important pattern does Nehemiah's prayer reveal to us?

6. Nehemiah had to overcome powerful fears. What were they? How do these fears relate to our own lives and circumstances?

CHAPTER 8: PREPARING FOR ACTION

1. Although Israel's enemies (Sanballat, Tobiah, and Geshem) didn't attack them as they rebuilt the walls, they engaged in a different kind of oppression. What was it? How does this kind of opposition affect us?

2. What is one way to prevent the world's scorn from affecting us?

3. What is the importance of the phrase "day and night" in Nehemiah's response to his enemy's threat? What are some of the examples the author gives to illustrate this principle? Can you give some others?

4. As God's people, where does our courage come from? What happens if we forget this?

5. How can we be sure that the God who protected the Israelites will protect us? Which of God's attributes assures us of his continued protection for his people today?

6. What do we need to do to develop a spiritual fight plan?

7. What two things must we do when faced with temptation? Why is setting goals important?

8. How does being in a small group help us overcome temptations? What is one essential component of sharing in a small group? Have you ever been a member of an accountability-oriented small group? How did it affect your spiritual life?

CHAPTER 9: PEOPLE OF ACTION

1. What are the first two steps of faith in action?

2. How does social justice relate to God's desires for his people? What is the biblical foundation of social justice?

3. What example illustrating social justice does the author give from his own experience? What do you think about this example? Is it always "safe" to practice social justice? What parable does Jesus use to illustrate social justice?

4. What theme in the book of Amos grounded Israel's understanding of social justice?

5. Social justice is predicated on a particular belief. What is it? Does it still apply today?

6. What are some of the barriers we encounter in putting our faith into action? Have you ever experienced any of these doubts and fears? What did you do about them?

CHAPTER 10: CONNECTIONS WITH THE LORD OF HISTORY

1. When the author went on a mission trip to Mississippi with some young people from his church, what did they do near the end of their sojourn there? Do you think they did the right thing, or should they have tried to find a place of worship with their own denomination?

2. What does the author mean by a "calling"? Have you ever experienced a call from God? What was it like? How do you know it was from God and not just your own feelings?

3. What two men are often overlooked in the story of God's replanting his people in the soil of Jerusalem?

4. When did these two prophesy: at the beginning or near the end of Israel's exile? How did their messages differ from each other?

5. What four things did Haggai chart in his message?

6. What must we do to understand Zechariah's message?

7. What does the name Jeshua mean? What powerful allusions to the Messiah appear in Zechariah's writings?

8. According to the author, how does prophecy work?

Chapter 11: Living in Celebration

1. The author speaks of a "false ideal of 'Christian joy.'" What is this false ideal? How do we know it's not true? What is the reality of Christian joy?

2. How does the story of Ezra and Nehemiah illustrate this reality?

3. What were some of the specific hardships facing the returned exiles?

4. According to the author, what is true celebration?

5. What tricks to try to derail the rebuilding process did Sanballat have up his sleeve? What was Nehemiah's response to these? What was the result for Israel's enemies?

6. What was the basis for Israel's celebration? Do we often think of the law in the way the Israelites regarded it? If not, why not?

7. What did the Israelites have to do before they could fully enter into celebration?

8. What is a lament? What are its particular characteristics? What pattern does it exhibit?

9. What follows the lament? What four clear stages does the prayer of blessing exhibit?

CHAPTER 12: TESTAMENT TO JOY

1. What do you make of the illustration that opens this chapter? How can we enter into celebration in the midst of such horrific circumstances?

2. What lies beneath celebration? What is the difference between celebration and joy?

3. How does the vignette ending the chapter illustrate joy?

4. Have you had similar experiences in your own life illustrative of joy? Can you describe them?

5. What does the author compare joy to? Do you think this comparison is apt? Why or why not?

6. What happens "if we measure joy by the increments of happiness in this life"? What is our true source of joy?

References

ॐ

The American Heritage Dictionary of the English Language, 4th Edition. New York: Houghton-Mifflin, 2000.

Augustine. *City of God.* Ed. Vernon J. Bourke. Garden City, NY: Doubleday Image, 1958.

Bonhoeffer, Dietrich. *The Cost of Discipleship.* New York: Touchstone, 1995.

Cloud, Henry. *Changes That Heal.* Grand Rapids, MI: Zondervan, 1992.

Cloud, Henry, and John Townsend. *Boundaries.* Grand Rapids, MI: Zondervan, 1991.

Colson, Charles, and Nancy Pearcey. *How Now Shall We Live?* Wheaton, IL: Tyndale House, 1999.

Dickinson, Emily. "The Soul Has Bandaged Moments." *The Complete Poems of Emily Dickinson.* New York: Modern Library, 2004.

Eliot, T. S. *The Complete Poems and Plays: 1909–1950.* New York: Harcourt, Brace & World, 1952.

Foster, Richard J. *Celebration of Discipline: The Path to Spiritual Growth.* San Francisco: HarperSanFrancisco, 1988.

Frost, Robert. "Birches," *The Poetry of Robert Frost: The Collected Poems, Complete and Unabridged.* Edited by Edward Cunnery Lathem. New York: Henry Holt, 1975.

Hoezee, Scott. *The Riddle of Grace: Applying Grace to the Christian Life.* Grand Rapids, MI: Wm. B. Eerdmans, 1996.

Kelly, Thomas R. *A Testament of Devotion.* London: Hodder and Stoughton, 1943.

Kennedy, D. James. *Evangelism Explosion.* 4th Edition. Wheaton, IL: Tyndale House, 2002.

Lewis, C. S. *The Great Divorce.* New York: Macmillan Press, 1946.

———. *Mere Christianity.* New York: Simon and Schuster / Touchstone, 1996.

———. *The Screwtape Letters.* New York: HarperCollins, 1996.

Packer, J. I. *Knowing God.* Downers Grove, IL: InterVarsity Press, 1979.

Pearcey, Nancy R. *Total Truth: Liberating Christianity from Its Cultural Captivity.* Wheaton, IL: Crossway Books, 2004.

Plantinga, Cornelius, Jr. *Engaging God's World: A Christian Vision of Faith, Learning, and Living.* Grand Rapids, MI: Wm. B. Eerdmans, 2002.

———. *Not the Way It's Supposed to Be: A Breviary of Sin.* Grand Rapids, MI: Wm. B. Eerdmans, 1995.

Saint John of the Cross. *Dark Night of the Soul.* Translated by E. Allison Peers. Garden City, NY: Doubleday Image, 1959.

Smedes, Lewis. *Forgive and Forget: Healing the Hurts We Don't Deserve.* New York: HarperCollins Publishers, 1984.

Sproul, R. C. *The Holiness of God.* Wheaton, IL: Tyndale House, 1985.

Thoreau, Henry David. *Walden.* Edited by Paul Lauter. Boston: Houghton-Mifflin Riverside Editions, 2000.

Tolkien, J. R. R. *The Hobbit.* New York: Houghton-Mifflin, 1999.

———. *The Lord of the Rings.* New York: Houghton-Mifflin, 2002.

Warren, Rick. *The Purpose Driven Life.* Grand Rapids, MI: Zondervan, 2002.

Wolterstorff, Nicholas. *Reason Within the Bounds of Religion.* Grand Rapids, MI: Wm. B. Eerdmans, 1976.

Whitfield, Charles. *Healing the Child Within: Discovery and Recovery for Adult Children of Dysfunctional Families.* Deerfield Beach, FL: Health Communications, 1987.

Yancey, Philip. *Rumors of Another World: What on Earth Are We Missing?* Grand Rapids, MI: Zondervan, 2003.

Additional copies of *Not So Far from Home*
and other VICTOR titles
are available wherever good books are sold.

ℬᴒ

If you have enjoyed this book,
or if it has had an impact on your life,
we would like to hear from you.

Please contact us at:

VICTOR BOOKS
Cook Communications Ministries, Dept. 201
4050 Lee Vance View
Colorado Springs, CO 80918

Or visit our Web site:
www.cookministries.com

Victor®
The Bible Teacher's Teacher